BE DO I

FAMILY SUCCESS TRIANGLE

Who you have to be and what you have to do, to have everything you want

by
Bestselling Authors

ERIC M. WOHLWEND & LILA J. WOHLWEND

MVHL

For permission requests, write to the publisher, addressed "Attention: Permissions Coordinator," carol@markvictorhansenlibrary.com

Quantity sales special discounts are available on quantity purchases by corporations, associations, and others. For details, contact the publisher at carol@markvictorhansenlibrary.com

Orders by U.S. trade bookstores and wholesalers. Email: carol@markvictorhansenlibrary.com

Cover Design - Low & Joe Creative, Brea, CA 92821
Book Layout - DBree, StoneBear Design

Manufactured and printed in the United States of America distributed globally by markvictorhansenlibrary.com

MVHL

New York | Los Angeles | London | Sydney

ISBN: 979-8-88581-066-1 Hardback
ISBN: 979-8-88581-074-6 Paperback
ISBN: 979-8-88581-068-5 eBook
Library of Congress Control Number: 2022919203

Contents

Dedicated to Our Fathers

Jerome "Jerry" L. Augustine

March 15th, 1942-October 27th, 2004

My dad was many things: at home, a father; at work, a manager; and in his spare time, a carpenter. People would have described him as quiet and thoughtful. Inside, he was just a big kid that I had a lot of fun with. He died of Cancer before my kids were born, so they never got to meet or know him. My mom and I have told them stories about him, so that they know a little about their grandfather. They have gotten to see and use many of the things he built. My dad taught me many things, including the curiosity to learn, having the patience to strive for quality, and a love of life (especially plants). He had the ability to lead through inspiration, which I did not recognize until later in my life, long after he was gone. He had a natural curiosity for things, and was interested in what Eric and I were initially learning about investing. I wish he could have seen how far we have come. He would be very proud of our accomplishments and his grandchildren. I am truly blessed to have had such wonderful, supportive parents in my life.

Albert W. Wohlwend, DDS
April 27th, 1948-January 18th, 2021

My father earned the Bronze Star in the 173 Airborne as an infantry platoon sergeant in Vietnam in 1969-1970. He then came home and was the first person in his family, child 9 of 10, to get a college degree. He was a dentist in the small town I grew up in. He taught me a lot of things that helped me succeed in life. Some of the lessons were more fun to learn than others…

Foreword by Mark Victor Hansen

Every Mom and Dad wants to be a great parent. As parents we're all looking for the best ways to nurture our children to live optimal lives. As parents we focus on school, homework, athletics, social activities and in recent years, monitoring online interactions. As providers, parents focus on career, earnings, opportunities, and best business practices.

But is there a way to seamlessly weave these different aspects of our parental responsibilities together, that maximizes opportunities and makes life more fun for everyone?

Eric and Lila Wohlwend have written the definitive book on just how to do that.

They have created more time freedom, social freedom, and financial freedom for their family with their powerful blend of home school education, business acumen, money management, and sharing of life lessons through their love, leadership, and example.

Their sons Deven and Ethan are light years ahead of most adults in building wealth through investment, experiencing life through travel, and developing their own confident identities.

Each chapter of this book will give you specific tools and insights that every parent can use to shift the dialogue and the relationship with your children starting today.

Here's to your new family success adventure!

— **Mark Victor Hansen**

Prologue

ERIC'S BACKGROUND

I, like many first time parents, was afraid that I wouldn't be a good enough dad. I had some issues with my father growing up. There were years as a teenager that I did not even talk to, or visit, my dad. When my first child, Deven, was born, he did not see his grandfather for the first year of his life. I never set out to do this. I never intended to keep him away from his extended family. In fact Deven spent a night or two every week at my Mom's house. He spent so much time there that my wife, Lila, asked me once if we had shared custody with her.

It may have been my strained relationship with my father that caused me to wait until I was 32 to have my first child. When he was born I was determined to be a great father. My dad always taught me to be a little bit better father than he had been. He said that he was a little better than his dad. If we kept this going generation after generation someday our family would be perfect. Impatient as I am, I did not want to wait for someday. I decided that I would shoot for perfect this generation. If I failed, which I was certain to do, I would still be much closer than just a little bit better.

Many of the people I grew up with thought it was good to be "Comfortable." I was fine with comfort, but not when they used that as an excuse to stay where they were. It was as if they couldn't be comfortable if somehow they got rich. Their goal was to be comfortable at the exclusion of being rich. They would ask things like how much is enough? I saw this as the same type of self-limiting belief as being just a little bit better dad. I made the choice to shoot for perfect in all aspects of my life. Asking me how much do you want to grow your business is like asking me how good of a dad do you want to be? I could never stop attempting to be better at both.

Looking back, I find it odd that my dad told me to be a little bit better. My dad was a dentist and always told me that it didn't matter if I was a doctor or a trashman, as long as I was the very best trashman ever. These incongruent lessons made it difficult to achieve any goals. The better I did at one thing, the farther I seemed to get from another. It wasn't until years later I realized the true meaning of congruency. When I aligned my goals, everything in my life started working better and getting easier.

I do not want to say that my dad was a bad father. He, like us all, taught his kids what he thought they needed to survive. He told us that in the army he had 3 jobs. Being a light weapons specialist and explosive expert never really helped in the real world. But being a drill sergeant really helped raising kids. Perhaps that is why I ended up working with explosives and then being an instructor in the Army... The problem we all have is that we learn from the people who love us the most, and most of these people are hardwired to keep us safe and comfortable - not to help us thrive. The key is learning the difference between the lessons that keep us alive and the lessons that are still holding us back.

The year that Deven was born, one of my teachers taught me the true meaning of the word congruency. I have used that lesson to separate all of the lessons that I had learned in the past. I have attempted to divide them into lessons that help me grow and thrive and the ones that just keep me safe and secure. I hope that I have used congruency to teach both of my kids to be better people.

I have always taught my kids, Deven and Ethan, to strive to be the best at everything that they do. I have also taught them that they will constantly fall down or fail along the way. That doesn't matter as long as they get up one more time than they get knocked down. You can never truly fail unless you give up.

I have had many great mentors in the last forty years. From the store manager at one of my first jobs (Thank you Mr. Stewart) to some of the greatest speakers, writers and trainers in the world. There are too many to name here, but I hope to point them each out at later points in this book. So right now I'll just mention Mark Victor Hansen. Hundreds of people have asked for this book. Multiple mentors have told me to write this book, but Mark was the one who finally made me want to write it. Every time I am around him or even talk to him on the phone I can feel his energy and it makes us all just want to be better human beings. His energy makes you want to do more for the world. After twenty minutes on the phone with him yesterday, my wife and I spent hours brainstorming.

So to everyone who has helped make me a better person and everyone who has helped to raise my children…Thank you!

— **Eric M. Wohlwend**

ERIC'S CHAPTER OUTLINE

- What's holding you back? Identify it and admit it.
- Why do you need to do better? Find your why…your most important cause.
- Don't limit yourself to "Comfortable." Shoot for rich and successful.
- Choose to succeed. Yes, you can change your life with a choice. It is that simple. It is not easy at all… but it is simple to choose a way that supports you.
- Congruence= Make sure that your thoughts, words and actions match your goals.
- Get mentors. Do not try to recreate the wheel. Use the knowledge and experiences of others to guide you.

LILA'S BACKGROUND

My childhood growing up was amazing. My parents raised me to be responsible, mature, and trustworthy. We had a great relationship. Now, they weren't perfect. They could only teach me what they knew. Unfortunately, some of what they "knew" was not true. For example, my family moved several times because my dad was laid off from jobs. They truly believed that this was because he did not have a college degree. They told me that in order to succeed, I needed to make sure that I got my college degree.

I had not liked school. I liked learning, but what school taught me was to sit down, be quiet, memorize the information they gave long enough to pass a test, and then move on to the next grade. I played that game well, as I got A's and B's. It wasn't until I met Eric that I realized that playing the game well does not mean you understand or can use the information you memorized. He could actually apply what he learned better than I could, even though he didn't play the game as well as I did. He made connections between what he heard and things he knew from before. At first, I thought he was just brilliant. Then he told me how he was in special classes when he was young because he had problems reading. It was one teacher that made the difference in his learning. She taught him to read. It was a defining moment for him in learning how to learn.

That's when I assessed my own learning. I did research on learning and discovered that some people learn by seeing things, others by hearing things, and the majority by doing things. That's when I realized that I'm one of those people that has to do something to learn it. Reading in a book is OK, but until I apply it, I don't really understand it, so all those years spent memorizing facts out of a book for a test were a waste of time because I never used the information.

The physical is what made something stick with me and help me to connect the information to what I learned previously. This was a big changing moment for me.

I knew that, when I had kids, I wanted them to be able to learn however they needed to in order to actually understand and use information. I really wanted to homeschool, but I needed to convince Eric of why this made sense. Parents always have a lot of concerns about homeschooling, including us. Would the kids be anti-social? Would the kids be as smart as other kids their age? Were we as parents smart enough to teach our kids? How would we do what needed done? There had been discussions over all of our concerns. There were also benefits to homeschooling that we discussed. We could teach our kids what we wanted them to learn. We could teach the kids how they learn the best, and we could travel and keep school going (and interesting) for them.

In the end, it wasn't our discussions that had the biggest impact on Eric's agreement to homeschool. What won him over was meeting my two cousins, who had been home-schooled their entire life. When he saw how bright, outgoing, and mature these young women were, he agreed to homeschooling our children. My cousins dispelled every myth, problem, or concern he had when he talked to them about their experiences being home-schooled. So that decision had been made.

I think this decision was key to the success of our children. Homeschooling gave us the freedom to teach our children what we wanted, when we wanted, and how we wanted, and the results were spectacular! What we taught them, we taught with the purpose of giving them everything they needed to succeed when they grew up. In my opinion, the purpose of parenthood is to make your children self-sufficient. Every lesson we taught had this end goal in mind.

As we raised our children, they watched us investing and building businesses. Both children chose to start investing themselves at a young age. By the time they were seven, they had bought their first investment property. This success has caused many other parents and investors to ask us HOW we made this happen. This book is to help answer those questions. What is fascinating is that some of these same lessons that helped our kids achieve amazing results have also helped Eric and I run businesses successfully. No matter whether you are looking for concepts to help your children be successful or concepts to help you with your business success, this book is for you.

We've had a lot of support over the years, including Deven and Ethan's grandparents, the Real Estate Investing Association members we spent time with, and many others that will be mentioned later in this book. I think all of this support helped us to achieve a much higher level of success. Thank you to everyone who has believed in us and helped us along our journey!

— Lila J. Wohlwend

LILA'S CHAPTER OUTLINE

- Just because your friends and family love you does not mean that they are giving you good advice.

- Memorizing is not learning.

- Most people do not really learn until they do something.

- There are many ways to learn and teach. Choose the one that is best for the student.

- Homeschooling gave us the freedom to teach our children what we wanted, when we wanted, and how we wanted.

- The lessons we learned running businesses helped us raise our kids and raising our kids helped us make our businesses stronger.

HOW ERIC & LILA GREW UP

We both grew up in middle class families. Eric's family was very poor until his dad graduated from dental school. Eric was 4 when his dad graduated and they moved to a small town in Ohio. Lila came from Kansas. Her dad lost a job and then got another near Chicago. This happened again and she ended up in Ohio. Both of our parents taught us to get good grades, go to college, and get a degree so we could get a good job. We did this. We both graduated with pre-med degrees from Kent State University. We both learned to stay out of debt. Lila was taught to save money. Eric was taught to save and invest in the stocks, bonds and mutual funds. When neither of us could find a job working with our degrees, we started looking for a better way. Lila continued to work in a hospital and then in an animal hospital for a couple years after graduation. Eric worked in the Emergency Room as a medic/EMT. Then, he got a job teaching Anatomy and Physiology at a high school. Finally he was activated by the Army after 9-11. During that activation, he started reading books on business and investing. Lila also started learning about these things.

A few months later we bought our first single family rental home. Two years later, when Eric was thirty and Lila was twenty-eight, we were financially free. We continued to learn and grow. We continued to use debt to buy cash-flowing assets. We also had two children and taught them about business and investing. In the past two decades, we have repositioned over a thousand units. We currently control many hundreds of rentals. We own, or have owned houses, apartments, mobile home parks, stores, a storage facility and part of an airport. We invest in precious metals, cryptocurrencies and oil wells.

We have made raising and teaching our children the main focus of our lives. We have started and grown many businesses. We have also written one best-selling book so far.

In between trips to their grandparents, the beach and other fun spots, the kids have started their own businesses. Now Deven is fifteen. He controls over forty units in multiple properties that he purchased with creative financing. He is the Best-Selling Author of *The Garage* and wrote a non-fiction book *If I Can Do It So Can You - How I Started Buying Real Estate at Age 7*. Ethan is twelve and controls over thirty units. He is currently writing his first book, *The Treehouse*. Both of them have been through enough real estate education to graduate and earn the title of Ohio Professional Housing Provider. They are the only two people who have completed this education before they were eighteen.

Both children have purchased their properties without any of their parents money. Neither Eric nor Lila has ever signed for a bank loan on any of these properties. All we did was teach our kids how we started buying real-estate without using our own money. We found that the traditional middle class beliefs of getting a degree and getting out of debt did not work for us. We found that the traditional school system seemed to want to make people more specialized and less self-sufficient. This had not worked for us and we refused to teach this to our kids. We knew that we would have to teach our kids about business and investing at home. We ended up teaching everything at home. Actually, home school is a misnomer. We taught our kids on vacation. We taught when we drove. We taught everywhere in every fun way we could come up with.

The results are the reason we are writing this book. We have taught our kids to start and run businesses before either child was old enough to drive. The kids have learned how to buy real estate without using their, or their parents' money. The whole family has traveled all over the US,

Canada and Mexico learning and teaching. Everywhere we go someone asks us, "How did your kids do that?" Here is our answer.

We knew that we could not possibly do all of the things we wanted to do in the traditional school system. It did not teach our values or the lessons that we wanted our children to learn. Eric tried working in the school system. We both tried working on the school system. We concluded that the system cannot be changed. We decided to build a system that is so much better that it will replace the current system.

Our goal in life is to make this world a better place. Every night we have told our kids that we love them and to dream about making the world a better place. We think you can make your world better, too. You can make the lives of everyone around you better by starting and growing a business. You can give jobs to others who need them rather than taking a job somewhere. We started by teaching this to our own kids. Then we taught to many other students of all ages. We are writing a curriculum for parents who think the traditional school system needs more financial education. When enough people take responsibility for their own lives and when they learn and teach others financial education, the world will be a better place.

OUR DECISION TO BUILD A NEW SYSTEM

- We knew that we could not possibly teach our children about business, investing, the big picture, working together and building a team and then send them to learn to work alone and memorize things in the traditional school system. It would be completely incongruent.

- Schools did not teach our values or the lessons that we wanted our children to learn.

- We concluded that the traditional school system cannot be changed. So we decided to build a system that is so much better, it will replace the traditional school system.

- Our children are our results.

A WORD FROM DEVEN

The way I grew up wasn't too much different from other kids. I still played, I still had school, and I still had friends. My parents just taught me different things than public school, especially in relation to time and money.

I have been home-schooled my whole life. One of the parts of my school was that I was rewarded for results, not time. Instead of just going to school, sitting down, and then leaving when they said I could, I just worked until I was done with however much I had to do that day. So, if it took me all day to complete my work, then I worked until the end of the day. But if I finished, no matter what time, then I was done and could play for the rest of the day. This meant I was always trying to be efficient with my work, which has helped me in several places since.

One day I decided to ask what normal school was like.

My mom started going through a regular day, and she didn't even make it past the time I would have to wake up before I told her that I was very happy with homeschool and did not want to go to public school.

When I joined a new Boy Scouts troop, I told some of the other scouts about the things I had done in my life. No one there knew that I owned real estate or had written a book. Most of them probably didn't believe me, and any of them that did probably just thought I was weird. From my point of view, it was normal. I had been learning about this stuff since I was born, and now I was actually using it.

When people hear that I wrote a book, they can't understand why a kid would ever want to do that. It seems so crazy to them that someone, especially a ten year old, would ever want to write a book. I don't look at it that way. I was just doing what I had done for fun previously. Then I figured out how to turn it into something that could help many more people.

I wrote my first book when I was roughly three years old. It was three pages long and only had one word in it, my name, which is the only word I could write at the time. A few years later, when I was five, I wrote a book on dragons. This book, while still short, was a drastic improvement from my first book. I don't remember why I decided to write a book, I just remember that I really liked the creative part of it. That was what got me interested in writing books. Writing my book on dragons showed me that I could create a story in my mind with nothing but a few easy concepts and some imagination. Then I could write it down so I wouldn't forget it. I liked that I could show other people what I had made. Then, years later, when I was at OREIA I heard a speaker who was offering his publishing course. I thought this could be an opportunity, not only to have fun writing another book, but I could also use that book to help teach people. I also thought it would be cool to be a published author.

Publishing that book helped me meet and become friends with the best-selling author in the world, Mark Victor Hansen, which is awesome. Mark Victor Hansen was the person who got me to publish my second book, *"The Garage"*. That book was a #1 bestseller the second day it was out.

All of these things have made my life very exciting and fun so far. I write books. I buy real estate and oil wells. I travel… AND I still get to go and play with my friends. I still get to see my grandparents all the time. I still get to spend time with my family. I do all of the important things that other kids my age do. I just chose to give up a lot of TV and video games so I could do some much bigger and more important things.

— **Deven J. Wohlwend, O.P.H.P.**
Bestselling Author of *The Garage*

A WORD FROM ETHAN

"Why did you start to invest?" People ask me that all the time. I started investing because my parents and brother were already investing, and told me investing was the reason we had the freedom and money to go where we wanted, when we wanted. I like to travel. I also really like that it will give me a lot more freedom when I turn 18 and move out. Passive income sounds way more fun than working every day at a job.

When I started I didn't think that investing in real estate would take that much time out of my day. Investing did take up more time than I thought it would, but I still had plenty of time to play with my parents and grandparents while keeping up with my business and school. Another reason I got to spend so much time with my grandparents was homeschooling. Yaya helped teach me English and PaPa let me work in the workshop with power tools. I used to go to my grandparents 3 days a week when I was younger. I saw my one grandma "Yaya and Poppy" almost every Sunday night until Tuesday. Then on Friday PaPa and Grandma Kathy would pick my brother and me up for the day.

School is taking more time since I got into harder classes in junior high. So I've started to go my grandparents less as I get older. After I started to spend more time at Boy Scout campouts and started speaking at business events it was too hard to keep up with schoolwork and still go to my grandparents that much. But I still see them about every other week.

Even though I am playing a lot of the time, and doing things at my grandparents' house that my dad probably would not let me do, I still have managed to grow my businesses a huge amount, and now I am starting to write a book series.

A lot of people think all I do is business, but I don't. I love riding my 4-wheeler on the farm. When I have to mow the farm, I at least get to ride the zero-turn mower. I play in the pond and have friends over for campouts. Even when I go to a business event, afterwards I usually talk to people, then go see if the swimming pool is open. Sometimes the people I meet are around my age and we become friends. I am still friends with some of the people I have met at these events years ago. If they live a long ways away, Dad flies me there to see them sometimes.

Some people think that I might not like going to business events, but I actually really like it because I get to fly in my dad's airplane. If I want, I even get to be the copilot. I get to go swimming. I get a break from the cold by going to events in Florida and Texas during the winter. One big bonus of going to all of these events is that I get to see different parts of the country. When I went to Rapid City South Dakota, I saw Mt Rushmore. I wouldn't have gotten to see Mt. Rushmore if it weren't for my parents taking me to the Red Pill Expo.

I know my life is not completely "normal" but I like it!

— **Ethan A. Wohlwend, O.P.H.P.**
Author of *The Treehouse*

We are not lawyers, accountants, financial advisors or perfect parents. These are just our opinions.

MYTHS & FAQ'S:

- As far as we have found, and Deven did a lot of research, It is not illegal for a minor to own real estate in any of the fifty states.

- It is legal for a minor to sign a contract. It is not enforceable until they follow the conditions of the contract after they turn eighteen. Think of a sixteen year old signing for a car.

- There is no difference between a sixteen year old and a seven year old in the eyes of the law.

- Our children do not own real estate in their names. No investor should own real estate. Our children own limited liability companies that own real estate. In our opinion, you should do it that way also.

- Home schooling is not illegal...but it was until recently in many areas.

- Homeschooling does not make children anti-social. Seriously, have you ever met our kids! Upbringing from role models: parents, grandparents, teachers, friends and even TV and video games makes kids what they are. It is not WHERE they learn. It is WHAT they learn that helps them develop into the people they are today.

- No, we never funded any part of any deal either of our children bought. What would that teach them?

- No, we never applied for or signed for a bank loan for either of them.

- No, we are not "cheating" the IRS. There are no tax advantages for kids owning real estate other than what we adults get. In fact we found out that there is a "Kiddie Tax" which is a punitive tax on them.

- Yes, there are multiple private lenders and creative strategies that minors can use to buy Real Estate. We will cover some of them in this book.

- Yes, the first child became a self-made millionaire, without our money or credit before he could drive.

- Yes, they really did all that you are about to read about and more. Just ask some of the thousands of people that have met them, heard them speak, their lenders, title companies, buyers, sellers and of course their friends that have watched them grow their own real estate empires since they were about seven years old.

CHAPTER 1

How People Learn and the Big Picture

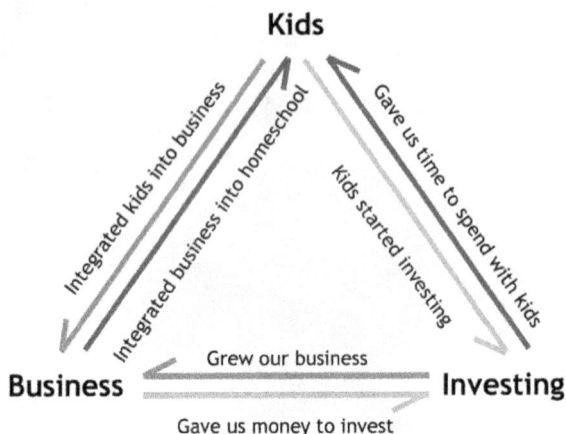

Kids

Integrated kids into business
Integrated business into homeschool
Gave us time to spend with kids
Kids started investing

Business ← Grew our business → **Investing**

Gave us money to invest

ERIC'S EXPERIENCES

At the last conference we were at, a man asked me, "How did you make your kids do all of that?" That answer is easy…You don't. After raising them to be as independent as they are, they would resent me for making them do something. As they should. Sure, they mow the lawn and take out the trash. But you cannot make your ten-year-old want to sit down and spend the better part of a year writing a book. To do something spectacular, you must first want to do it. You must have the right motivation.

Children are creative and motivated. They always want to try new things. They always want to learn more. I remember hearing that awful saying "The Terrible Twos." I never had that experience. When my children were around two, they learned to talk. Like many other two-year old's their favorite question was "Why?" I loved it. I could finally start explaining some of the great mysteries of the world to my own son. Unfortunately, when he asked about why is the sky blue, he was not interested in the refraction of light waves through vaporized water molecules in the air. That is when I realized that you need to teach at a level that is just above their understanding. That way they continue to learn and grow but are not completely lost. I also learned that the way we frame a situation will frequently dictate how it will end. So, every time someone mentioned the "Terrible Twos" I corrected them. I told them it was the "Terrific Twos."

It was even before the Terrific Twos that I remember Lila calling me into the living room. She told me that Deven knew his colors. It wasn't that I didn't believe her. It was just that he couldn't talk yet. I thought that made it much harder to give him a test on the colors. As Lila mentioned earlier, I had issues learning as a kid. I was in second grade and could not read at all. It was not until Mrs. Askren took special interest in me. She tutored me every evening and gave me extra homework from first grade workbooks to help me get caught up with the rest of the class. She taught me how to read. But more than that she taught me how to learn.

It was not just sit down, shut up and memorize this. She showed me how things fit together. Other than the people I am related to, she created more value in my life than any other person. She not only taught me to read; she taught me to learn. In college I could read over 100 pages of text a day and remember the page an answer was on. I have read more than a thousand books in the last couple decades: biographies, how-tos, and sometime just military or medical fictions. None of this would have been possible without her support. Once I learned how to put things together, life became much easier.

When I did my first year at Kent State, there was a girl in the lab across from me. She was a couple years older than the rest of us eighteen-year old's. She had worked in a pharmacy for years. She knew things that we had never heard of. It was such an unfair advantage. She used her knowledge from work to help her in school. That was one of the reasons that I wanted to be a medic in the Army. So I could have that unfair advantage in medical school. It is also how I teach my children. I do everything I can to give them an unfair advantage. Looking at that term, is it really unfair if they do all of the work to learn it?

Everything we do in our lives can be looked at as broken and disjointed. We can keep memorizing things and make no connections to other lessons that we have learned. Or we can step back. See the big picture and see how these pieces fit together. Even if you can't see it when it is happening to you, there is a reason that you are going through what you are today. It is likely that you will need the lessons that you are learning to make it through, or to thrive tomorrow. My religious mentors would say everything happens for a reason. God doesn't give you more than you can handle. And if you do not complete this lesson successfully today, I promise you will get a chance to overcome an equivalent obstacle later in life. In other words you might as well learn and grow now. If you do not, you will continue to have the same problems throughout the rest of your life.

Remembering that there are many different ways to learn, I figured that Lila was not giving our seven-month-old a written test before he could speak. I found them both sitting in the living room with four colored squares. Lila would hold up two and ask him to pick out the yellow one or the red one. When he picked the correct one every time, I was excited. Not because he knew his colors. But because he had learned enough words to understand what he was being asked to do. He then had the hand eye coordination to reach out and grab the correct square. AND he knew and could choose the correct color. I realized then that these little human beings comprehend WAY more than we give them credit for. From then on, I talked to him as if he could understand more complex subjects. Sure, I always break things down to the simplest level, but I still teach complex subjects to any of the younger kids that I meet.

I have a saying. "A Ph.D. can teach fourth grade math using calculus. But it takes a genius to teach calculus using fourth grade math." Everyone you meet has the capacity to understand things that are well above their education level. If we cannot get our point across, it is not their ability to understand that is the problem. It is our ability to teach the subject that is lacking. While my wife and I both have B.S. degrees (I mean Bachelor of Science); we still teach at the fourth grade level whenever possible.

I have never met an adult that completely understands how the credit bureaus arrive at your credit score. I have been in many classes that teach you what is important and how to improve your credit. Other than pay your bills on time, every one of them has a different formula for increasing your credit score. So, if none of these "Experts" can agree on exactly what to do, why should we think that we know exactly what to do. If we don't know, then how can we teach our students or children? That being said, neither Deven nor Ethan are eighteen yet. Neither of them has a credit score. But both of them have hundreds of thousands of dollars of loans from people who believe they are credit worthy.

When I wanted them to learn about credit, I stepped back. I saw the big picture. I realized that as employers, landlords and lenders, we only want to see that number that is called a credit score to see if someone is generally trustworthy. We want to use it to speculate on whether they will pay their bills. We want to see if they are a good bet to loan money to, or to rent to. If the powers that be assume that you cannot build credit until you are eighteen, I want to question that assumption. I want to skip to the bottom-line.

I taught my kids to be trustworthy. I taught them the value of the dollar and, more importantly, of their word. I had them get checking accounts when they were ten or twelve. That, by the way, was way harder than their buying a house at seven. They learned that when they sign their names on that check, they better have the money in the account. They learned to pay their bills on time. They also learned what a responsibility it was to safeguard someone else's retirement. They may quote Spiderman "With great power comes great responsibility." But they do understand that many of their lenders worked and saved their whole lives to get enough money to finance a couple houses for them. They understand what an honor it is to be trusted with that much. They learned that what was once an unimaginable amount of money to them may be a small amount to us adults. And they also have grown to see that what is now just one more house to them represents the life savings of many others.

The true value of money is different for everyone. It is not until you cherish every dollar that you are worthy of receiving more. Harv (T. Harv Eker, one of my mentors) says that if you can't handle what you have, you won't get any more. He and Mark Victor Hansen both talk about being a Money Magnet. My kids grew up with this. They even have shirts that say, "I am a Money Magnet." If you teach your kids that money is bad, or it is the root of all evil, why would they ever want to have any money. Almost all people want to be good. You cannot pay your rent or buy food for your family without money. Can you explain to me how not having money makes you good? So, who is the better person? The one who pays their bills as they agreed to or the one being evicted?

This is the lesson that many rich philanthropists taught

me. By the way, have you ever met a poor philanthropist? What I also learned is that you must be congruent. You cannot say one thing and wish for or get another. If you keep doing this, it will cause nothing but heartache and pain in your life. If you don't have enough money today, look at your feelings and beliefs about money. If you don't have enough time with your family today, look at your priorities. If we can run the multiple businesses that we own, manage hundreds of rentals, homeschool our children, write books, go to Boy Scouts, and still travel about six months a year, I am sure that you can find a good work/family balance.

These are two of the biggest lessons I have attempted to teach my children. Be congruent and make sure you have a good balance in life. Just last week my twelve-year-old chose to do way more history assignments and way less math. He needs more balance in school. It is easy to do more of what you like. Or even what you see as the last emergency. Stop looking back. Look to the future. Don't look at what you are lacking. Look for what you will need for the next stage of your life. When I joined the Army, we were still wearing the same leather boots they had in WWII. We were still training to fight in Vietnam. It is human nature to prepare for the past. It doesn't matter if you are in junior high or a general in the pentagon. Every one of us needs to start preparing for the future, rather than the past.

I find that the more school people go to, the more specialized they get. I remember when my dad use to clean teeth and pull them when needed. Now, you need a referral and a specialist to get anything done. I thought that when I grew up, I may need to know an attorney. I had no idea that I would need one for evictions, one for collections, one for litigation, one for lobbying…I have taught my kids to go the other way. Rather than being more specialized than anyone, I helped them to learn to see a bigger picture than anyone else. They can always hire the highly trained specialists that got better grades than me when they are needed. One of my favorite quotes is by Robert A. Heinlein.

A human being should be able to change a diaper, plan an invasion, butcher a hog, conn a ship, design a building, write a sonnet, balance accounts, build a wall, set a bone, comfort the dying, take orders, give orders, cooperate, act alone, solve equations, analyze a new problem, pitch manure, program a computer, cook a tasty meal, fight efficiently, die gallantly. Specialization is for insects.

— Robert A. Heinlein

Once you teach your children to see a bigger picture and to act congruently you will just have to get out of their way. Then you can sit back and watch their greatness. But that is a story for another chapter.

ERIC'S CHAPTER OUTLINE

- You cannot make anyone do anything for long. They have to want it.

- Children are insatiable learners. Don't try to stop them; encourage them.

- Knowing how to read is not an advantage unless you actually do read.

- You can see pieces, or you can see how they fit together. Every individual thing that we learn is preparing us for the next bigger task.

- Your words and actions do create your results. Think, speak, and act in ways that get you closer to your goals.

- To be truly successful you must balance work, family and money.

- Highly educated people get more specialized for their jobs. Business owners focus on the big picture and hire specialists.

LILA'S LESSONS

I remembered my parents reading to me a lot as a kid. That gave me a love for reading, and I wanted to give that to my children as well. So, like a lot of parents, I read to my kids even before they were born. While a lot of people told me that the kids won't understand what I am reading – that they will only learn my voice – I was selective about what it was that I chose to read to my unborn child. I remembered the line from the movie *Good Will Hunting* where he said that people read the wrong books. I wanted to read the right ones to my children. One of the kid's books that I chose to read frequently was Dr. Seuss's *Oh the Places You'll*

Go. Eric's choice was to read *Atlas Shrugged*, which was not quite as age appropriate but still a great book!

After my kids were born, I continued to read to both of them. It was part of the learning I wanted them to have. I took every opportunity to teach them something. Diaper changing time was the time to sing songs about the alphabet, numbers, and colors. Bath time was a time to sing about animals and water. I also tried very physical experiences, like having them touch items with different textures and feels. I was trying to determine how they would learn the best.

With Deven, I realized that he was watching the pages of books as I read them, even as an infant. I started to move my finger under the words I was reading, and he would follow my finger as well as look at the pictures. This told me that he was a visual learner. So, then I tried something crazy. I got out flash cards and showed them to my infant. He would watch the flash cards as I went through colors, shapes, letters, and numbers. The colors seemed to be his favorite. He was around seven months old when I started quizzing him on colors. I would hold up two colored squares and ask him which one was blue. Then I would take his hand and put it on the blue one. He caught on to this game. Then I could ask the question and he would put his hand on the correct color.

One day, after about twenty minutes of playing this game, we showed Eric what we had learned. Eric was amazed that a child less than a year old could tell his colors.

We grabbed the video camera to record this, but by then Deven was getting bored with the task. We still captured the moment, even though he squirmed and didn't pay as much attention. Deven had just proved that kids learn more than adults expect.

Deven also surprised me when I was painting at a rental house. Back then, I didn't realize how much better it was to hire people to do these things, so I was still too hands-on with my investments. I had Deven in a pack-and-play in the living room, and I was painting in the bedroom around the corner. In between us, I had the CD player sitting on the kitchen counter, with Blair Singer talking about sales. In between the different sections of the learning, there would be a pause and then the sound of dogs barking, indicating the change to a new section. After a few rounds of this, as soon as the pause began, there was a barking sound from the other room, even before the CD dogs barked. I stopped painting and went into the living room. Deven had barked along with the CD. He was LISTENING with me! He wasn't really talking yet, but he was paying attention to what was around him. That was when I realized that he could learn the same things I was learning. Perhaps, as a baby, he wouldn't understand it all as well as I could, but the concepts would be there for him. We could learn together.

People had already been impressed with how young Eric and I had gotten started investing. We were the youngest people at our local Real Estate Investors Association

(REIA). I was twenty-six when I started. I thought that if Deven learned while I was learning, perhaps he would get started at eighteen. Wouldn't that be great? From that point forward, I just included him on anything I was learning. He went to REIA meetings, investment breakfasts, and conferences with Eric and me. He was a happy, quiet baby, and if there was something to hold his attention, he was incredibly well-behaved.

We also let him make his own decisions, even before he could talk well. After seeing Eric tell a server to ask Deven what he wanted to eat and Deven pointing to the picture in the menu of what he wanted, I knew this would be an important piece of learning. Kids need to learn that they can make a decision, and that every decision has an outcome. That outcome might be positive or negative, as he sometimes really liked the food he ordered and sometimes he didn't. No matter what he ordered, that's what he had to eat. This was a great way to teach him to make good decisions. He also learned later to ask our opinion on whether he would like a new food item. He learned that sometimes talking to someone who had already tried something could help him make a better decision.

Then we found out we were expecting a second child. Ethan was different from his brother even before he was born. He never stopped moving, which made it difficult for me to sleep. After he was born, he was loud, boisterous, talkative, and demanding as a baby. Trying to sing during diaper time or bath time was difficult, as he wanted to be the one talking or singing. He had no interest in flash cards. They were just things he wanted to grab at. He tried to pick up everything. By the time he could crawl, which he did earlier than his brother, he was into everything. It was frustrating, as Deven had been such an easy baby. When my mom mentioned that he was just like me, I realized the problem. He was one of those kids that learned by doing.

From that point on, all learning was a physical endeavor. Learning letters was done with blocks that had letters on them. Numbers were done with blocks or a certain number of toys that he could pick up. I had to get very creative on teaching things, as both children learned very differently.

Deven learned how to read by listening to me read to him and watching my finger slide under the words I was reading. Ethan bounced the entire time he was learning to read. I learned that if he had something to hold in his hand, he could bounce and look at a page with some degree of focus. However, focus was a lot harder for him than it was for Deven. I was glad we were homeschooling, as the regular school system may have put a label on him or asked us to drug him. I didn't want that for him. He just needed a different way to learn.

Going to investment meetings with Ethan was next to impossible in the beginning. They were too much like regular school where you sit down, stay quiet, and listen to the person speaking. There was not enough physical activity at those events to keep him interested. I felt like a bad mom leaving him at home, and I had to get really creative to try to tell or teach him about anything I had learned while we were away. We did keep the CD's playing at home while he was doing something to integrate our investment learning with movement.

Deven was probably the best teacher for Ethan. The two were inseparable as young kids. Deven seemed to communicate with Ethan the easiest, and he would talk to his brother about a lot of different things he was learning. They would sit around, building things with Legos, and talk about anything and everything. It was heartwarming to watch the two of them together.

Family time included playing the game Cashflow, by Robert Kiyosaki. We played every Friday night, and friends would usually join us. Deven figured out how to add, and he started joining in the game. Ethan would sit with us, play with extra pieces, and help move parts for us. It was a great learning and fun experience for all of us. Every week I learned something new. I hoped the kids were learning also. We planned to continue this for years and wanted both kids playing with us. This game was pivotal for all four of us in learning investing.

In the end, it was the game of Uno and Ethan's competitive nature that taught him math. He kept track of scores and would add points together. His desire to win at this game made learning math enjoyable for him. When he could add his points in his head, which he learned to do rapidly, we determined that he was ready to join in the Cashflow game also. His competitive nature also helped him in this game. Thanks to Eric giving him a lot of help in the game, he had only played it a handful of times before he made it out of the rat race before the rest of us. His love of learning investing had begun!

During one of the first REIA events we took him to, he brought pen and paper to take notes. During the meeting, his pen seemed to never stop. After the meeting, I looked at his "notes". There were a couple of words and phrases, but most of the pages were filled with doodles. At first, I was upset. Did he just sit and draw the whole time? However, then Eric was asking him questions about the things that were taught, and Ethan could answer every one of them. So, while doodling, he was taking in the information. The physical activity allowed him to focus on the presentation from the speaker. I knew that as long as he was learning, he would never get chastised for drawing pictures on his notes. This was what he needed to do to learn.

Having two children that learn differently taught me a lot about the differences between kids' learning needs and why some kids have an easier time in regular school than others. Being able to homeschool our children allowed both of them to learn how they learn the best. Deven needed to see something to understand it. Once the mental picture was in his head, he had it. Ethan needed to do it to understand it. Once his muscles understood it, so did his brain.

Understand that the people who work for you also learn in different ways. Training needs to be geared to different learning needs. Take some time to get to know the people you have hired, so that you can explain things in ways that they will understand. Not only do we teach our kids in different ways, we teach our kids that there are different ways to teach. We knew the kids would need to know this when they were running their own businesses or raising their own children.

I wished I had been home-schooled and learned like Ethan. I think I would have been better off from a learning standpoint. However, after learning to get creative to teach Ethan things, I have also learned ways that I can learn better. Now, sometimes even my notes have doodles on the side, as when my thoughts start to stray, I can bring myself back to focus with the movement of the pen. It is amazing what we can learn from our children.

LILA'S CHAPTER OUTLINE

- You and your children learn when you read to them.
- Every time is a good time to teach and learn.
- People learn in all different ways. Teach in the way they learn best.
- Allow them to make decisions. Then let them live with the consequences, good or bad.
- You can learn a lot playing games like Cashflow 101, Monopoly...even Uno.
- Some people NEED physical action to learn and remember. You have to let them move, doodle or

bounce sometimes. They are not paying less attention to you. They are paying more attention.

- Home-schooling allows you to pick the way your
kids learn best. Traditional school forces all children
to learn the same way.

CHAPTER 2

Balance & Integration: Family, Work & Money

ERIC'S EXPERIENCES

I was determined to be the best father in the world. Like I said before, I knew that no one can be perfect. But that is no excuse to not try to be perfect. There are so many decisions to make when you are new parents. Some people take the big things for granted. Don't do that. Question everything.

Two weeks before Deven was born, I decided that I wanted to speak for Peak Potentials Training. Lila and I had both been through every course that they offered, and it had changed our lives. I wanted to be part of that training for others. I understood that it was a huge time commitment. I also guessed that a new baby was going to take up a lot of my time. I was right on both accounts. At the time I had no idea how "Right" I could be. Both took far more time and money than I anticipated.

So, to get started, I let the company know that I wanted to be one of their next trainers. They very clearly told me no. I said that I would continue to volunteer to work for them for free until I proved my value. The person I was talking to went so far as to tell me that if I showed up at their next event in Florida, they would not let me in. So, with my first son due in two weeks, I jumped in a truck with a friend, and we drove from Ohio to Florida. I believed that the first child always comes late so I had plenty of time to drive a thousand miles, volunteer at a three-day seminar and then drive back home before Lila went into labor.

We made it there, and they let us in. It turns out that they did not have nearly enough help at that event. They even called and asked if I could come help out the day it started. Thankfully I was in the right place at the right time. It only took a risk of driving a thousand miles to get there. The timing was not perfect, but it all worked out perfectly in the end. At the end of that event, I ended up getting sicker than I think I had ever gotten before. JC, who became Deven's godfather, got stuck driving the whole way home. And yes, I did make it home in plenty of time for my first child's birth.

I continued to show up at these events and was told I didn't have enough experience speaking or teaching. Apparently being a skydiving instructor wasn't the type of experience they were looking for. As soon as they said this, I started scheduling more speeches at local Real Estate Investment Associations (REIA's.) Finally, I started to be noticed by the higher-ups, and they asked me to be in Scottsdale two days later. Harv himself wanted to see me onstage. Apparently, they had a couple hundred other people that also wanted the trainer's job. Out of the original 200-300, they had cut it down to about thirty. I was invited to tryout with those thirty.

It turns out that the Army had trained me well to drop everything and travel halfway across the country, or to another country, with no notice. Something about the 18-hour recall at Ft. Bragg that makes two days seem like plenty of time. Unfortunately, I was doing what I was told to do. I was getting more experience training. I had scheduled something the night they wanted me there. After completing my scheduled engagement and then catching a red-eye I made it in the morning of the second day. Harv seemed completely unimpressed that I had missed more than half of the two-day event. I was told that we were presenting four different lessons. I was prepared to do all four back-to-back. I had memorized them on the plane ride there.

They put me on stage shortly after I got there. I had a feeling that I did not stand out after my last presentation. About that time Harv asked something about selling. I'm not sure what all I said, but I remember quoting how many sales I had made for his company in the past couple events. I also remember telling him I got more out of his events than a 4-year degree. I told him that when my kids were old enough to go, I would rather send them to his seminars than to college. I was sure that it would be better for them. Apparently, it worked. He asked me for my card, and then I started training with him and his company to be one of their trainers.

It is one thing to say that you will go against the common beliefs of the general public and all of your family. It is another thing to do it. I really believed that this was the best way to educate my children. I don't have any idea why I didn't also see that an alternative method of schooling, like home school, could also be far superior to the traditional system. Lila had to show me that. Now, here we are about fifteen years later. Both of my kids have gone to Harv's Millionaire Mind Intensive, George Gammon's Rebel Capitalist, the Limitless Expo, REIA groups and conventions all across the US, Canada and Mexico. They have been to so many others I can't count them all. Based on the results that every twenty-five to thirty-year-old college graduate that I know is getting, I made the right choice.

I had the incredible opportunity to work with Harv and his staff for about a year. At one time, I spent almost every waking moment for two weeks directly with Harv, Dennis and Kieron, driving around British Columbia, teaching multiple classes. I also became good friends with Robert Riopel. Thanks so much for all that you taught me, Rob!

Dennis high-fives Deven & Eric at one of Deven's first trainings.

At different times my baby, who I think was two months old at his first event, disappeared. One of the staff stole him. Next thing I knew he was in an "Expect Miracles" T-shirt, onstage, in front of over a thousand people. To Dennis, Kieron, Stewart, Dave, Seymour, and all the incredible staff at Peak Potentials, I want you to know that you not only changed my life forever. You improved the lives of my whole family. I hope that we can do the same for the whole next generation.

After about a year of this I was one of the assistant trainers and was spending more time on stage. I was getting everything I wanted out of life. Just a few years earlier I didn't even know that places like this, or people like this existed. Now I was in the middle of it. I was on stage. I was traveling back and forth from the US to Canada just like I commuted to the next town over for one of my last jobs. Every time I went home, I did nothing but play with my son. He sat on my lap every night until he fell asleep. I carried him upstairs. I told him I loved him and that he should dream about making the world a better place.

All of this seemed great. But then I realized that all I did was travel, speak and play with my son. I forgot to fit running my business into the equation. I had zero balance in that area. So, after realizing that I had just spent six months on the road of my son's first year of life, and seeing that my decisions were allowing my business to crash, I decided to stop right then. There was a bit of trouble in the real estate market that year, 2007-2008. It was causing many real estate companies and investors to go broke. I have never thought that a changing market was what caused my problems. I have always known that the decisions I made then led to my results. When I finally opened my eyes and saw how much my business had fallen, I knew I needed to do something to regain my balance.

For a while I told people I laid on the couch for a week crying and feeling sorry for myself. Then I looked back at my journal. It was more like an hour. By the end of my first day of working on balancing my life better, I had postponed what I thought would end in bankruptcy by a few days. I remember walking into my office, opening my email and then not stopping until 2 am. I also remember holding my son so tight, while I kneeled in front of the fire and prayed. I could feel the love flowing from my son to me. This is something I could not even imagine until I had kids of my own. This little baby that couldn't eat without help, gave me the strength I needed to keep going. At the time, I didn't understand balance nearly as well as I do now. But I did know that I needed this and that I would never be away from it again.

I have done a lot of exciting things in my life. When we got married, I asked Lila what she wanted out of life and our marriage. She said adventure. She should have looked at my resume first. Since then, we have made hundreds of skydives together, including many from over four miles high. We have been SCUBA diving through caves in the Caribbean over 100 feet below the surface. (Actually, I think Lila missed that dive, but she did do the shark dive with me.) As much as I enjoyed these things, nothing brought me as much happiness as speaking to large groups of people and helping them to grow and make their lives better. And yet, as much joy as that brought me, it didn't begin to compare to doing things that I love with my whole family.

When I walked away from speaking, I told people that I would start again when my children were old enough to travel with me. I did not know if that would ever happen. But I chose to be with my family first. People always say how fast kids grow up. They apparently don't remember all the nights when babies woke them up every other hour. Now, looking back at the last fifteen years I know I was always right where I was supposed to be. I never imagined that I would have a twelve and fifteen-year-old that would both share a stage with me and my wife. The last couple years I have been able to combine the best things in life. I never imagined that I would be on stage with my whole family. I also never thought I would write a book. It is amazing what happens when you are open to anything.

Since we started, we have spoken from Ohio to Florida, out west to Arizona and even down to Mexico. In every one of these places, people stop and ask, "How did you get your kids to do all of this?" I wish I had given every one of them a better answer. The thing is, there is no one answer. This book is my answer. We are writing whole chapters about what we think the most important answers are. But if you must pick just one answer…it is Balance!

I look back at all of the traveling I have done, and we

have done. I really have never missed a single important moment in my family's lives. And important moments in my family's lives have never taken away from my business or hobbies. At least after that first year. That is why I think Balance is the most important part of life. If you can't find the time for both, just remember that the world is infinitely abundant. Keep going. Try it a different way. Create a team. You can have everything you want. As Harv would say, "I Choose Both!"

If it is difficult to find the balance you want, focus on the present. Not the future or past. Take a few deep breaths. Clear your mind. When you focus on your breathing, it helps to bring you back to the present from whatever you were thinking about. This can help you focus on work when you need to. You can do this to forget about work and focus on your kids when you are with them. The worst way to try to find balance is to leave work at five o'clock, and then pretend that you are having family time while you worry all night about work. It is not better to go to work and worry about your kids all day. Be where you are. Live in the present. Do not worry about what may happen in the future.

> **"I've had a lot of worries in my life, most of**
> **which never happened."**
>
> **— Mark Twain**

Another way to have better balance in life is just to integrate all the important things into the same activities. You will see that we have plenty of time for everything in life because we integrate everything that is important in every part of our life. Sure, we have days that we only train and do not take calls from the real estate brokerage. We have times every day that we just sit and read together and never answer our phones. We take vacations to beautiful islands and mountains or wherever we want to go. We just take them with our whole family. And we generally attend a conference while we are there or invite people to have a mastermind. I was never a "sit on the beach and waste a day type of person." I would much rather be taking action. Learning and growing. I unwind every night, but it is not by going to the bar for a beer. It is by talking to my family and friends. Sometimes this is at a bar. Sometimes there is beer, but the end goal is not to escape from life. It is to discuss what happened in our day so we can celebrate each other's victories and help each other grow stronger than the problems that they experienced that day. And, like every family, we have times we just want to be alone. The kids may walk the dog or go to grandma's or just play with Legos. Lila likes crafts and puzzles. I like to go flying. When things seem to be getting out of control, I like to take total control of my life. I have not found a better way than to jump into (or out of, if there is another pilot) an airplane. Being able to pop above the clouds and see the sun at any time during a long dreary Ohio winter day gives me the energy to accomplish anything.

Find ways that you can integrate your hobbies into your businesses. Find ways to show your family the fun parts of what you do at work. When you are all working and playing together as a family, it does not take away from work or family time. It adds to both.

ERIC'S CHAPTER OUTLINE

- Strive to be the best, not just a little better.
- Question Everything.
- You will have to overcome many "No's" to get what you want.
- If you are not willing to risk doing the unknown, you will always be stuck where you are.
- If you lose sight of one of the important parts of your life, it can ruin all the good parts that you have been focusing on.
- Your decisions create your results.
- Money does not buy you a good family. A good family life does not make you rich. To really be successful, you have to focus on both.

LILA'S LESSONS

When Eric told me of his decision to work with Peak Potentials, I was excited. The things we had learned from those courses completely changed our life. Being able to give that to more people was very important. I wanted to see more people learn the things we were learning!

In our business and investments, Eric and I both had our roles. He did certain things better than I, so he handled those items, and I handled the items I was good at. However, when he left to teach and travel, I had to cover all the roles. At the time we only had a few people working for us. We had recently opened an office away from home and the people there really just did their one little piece of the work. There was no cross training or integration between jobs. We did not have a good systems manual written out at that point. So for some tasks, I had to guess how Eric had gotten them done. For a good portion of these items, I was totally unprepared to handle them. Some things I managed to make work, but others, I did very poorly. One of my biggest failures during this time was seeing the big picture.

Months later, Eric sat down with me, and we looked at our financial statement. We were in terrible shape at a time when the real estate market was crashing. I was devastated that I had let him down and couldn't figure out how to make it all work. He was upset that he hadn't caught the problem faster. After an hour or two of dealing with the understanding of how bad our situation was, Eric sat down at his computer. He came up with a plan, and we followed through on that. We made it through, were never a day late on a payment to anyone and learned some very valuable lessons from that difficult time. I learned that I needed to be able to see the big picture, and we both learned how important a systems manual would be to our future success. Then, anyone would be able to follow the system to get something done correctly every time. This became even more important as we hired more employees and contractors.

I also learned that I had no idea how to balance things. I was supposed to be a mom, take care of the things at home, run a business, make investments, hire people, manage people, and homeschool my child. There were days when work seemed to overwhelm everything else. Then I would try to make it up to my son the next day, but then the business wouldn't get the attention it needed. I tried to look for a mentor that could give me some insight on how to make everything work on a daily basis, but I couldn't find any books, speakers, or people near me that seemed to be able to help.

Going through that difficult time, I realized how important learning that balance really was. I also learned the importance of time. Each of us only has twenty-four hours a day to get everything done. We cannot do everything ourselves. We need to build a team that can help handle the day-to-day items so that we can focus on the other tasks that are a higher priority for our lives. Building a team became an important goal, and I knew I would have to learn better leadership skills in order to do this. Today I am still working to improve these skills, as I believe it may be the most important thing to improve both my life and the lives of those around me. My kids have watched my successes and mistakes in these areas over the years, and I hope that this has better prepared them to be good leaders.

I know that they are learning to balance the things in their lives. They balance work, school, investments, extra-curricular activities, writing books, and traveling to speak and teach at different events. Their lives are very busy, and they don't always get the balance right. However, they are learning good lessons about time management, planning, and balance. I believe these lessons will help them excel. They are also learning how to have fun by integrating seminars with vacations. Kids are great at finding ways to combine work and fun, just like Eric taught then to reconcile our accounts and taught them it was a game like Memory. They have found ways to make even the most boring tasks fun for themselves and everyone else around.

Life is like a teeter-totter on the playground. I remember sitting on one side and Deven trying to sit on the other. He was too small, so we didn't balance. Then Ethan joined him. Even with two of them on the other end, we didn't balance. Then I moved to sit past the handle, and we could balance, but the movement wasn't as smooth. However, when Deven sat on one side, Ethan on the other, and I sat in the middle, slightly closer to Ethan because he was smaller, we all balanced and had smooth movement. In life, sometimes we just have to arrange things, so they are all in just the right place in our lives. That way we can move smoothly and have balance.

Everything has its balancing point. For example, one that many people have problems balancing is their work life and their family life. If your work life is on one side of the teeter-totter and your family life is on the other side, it is up to you to be the one in the middle, sometimes leaning a little more toward getting work items done, so your business continues to grow and thrive. Other times you'll need to lean a little more toward your family life, so your kids and your relationships can continue to grow and thrive. If you do this right, things move and work smoothly. When they get out of balance, you need to correct quickly before one of them crashes to the ground.

Sometimes the order of things really helps with this. For example, I get up early in the morning, before any of my family is out of bed, so I can do things that I don't want distractions for: reading, work decisions, writing, etc. Then, when everyone else gets up, I can give them my attention. I like that our family eats breakfast together every morning. It is great to have a family moment, before we all start our projects for the day, whether that be work, school, or something else. Be sure that you take the time to enjoy moments that mean something to you.

Sometimes, you need to reallocate the weight. You can't be on all places on the teeter-totter at the same time. You need to be able to get help, assign the right person to the right area or task, and use your team to help balance everything. That was a big lesson for me.

In the beginning, this balance was really difficult for me. I was trying to do too much on my own, and all parts of my life were suffering. I would work crazy hours and then feel guilty that I wasn't spending enough time with my family. Then I would take time away from work to spend time with my family and feel guilty not being there for my team. It was a little like trying to run from one side of the teeter-totter to another, trying to keep it balanced. Then I wondered why I was so tired, and everything still seemed out of whack. I had a real problem letting go of work tasks and trusting my team members. I have improved on this greatly over time, but I am still working on letting go. Even now, when my world gets out of balance, it is usually from the same problems I had back then. Only now, I understand that I have large goals, like helping other families get started homeschooling, helping bring children financial education, and helping kids know that they can start their own business, even if they are under eighteen. In order to accomplish the things I want to do, I will need to let go so I can balance my life with these extra goals included.

We always teach that "If the Why is Big enough, the How will take care of itself." If you don't have time to grow your business, do you choose to wait to have kids until you get it under control? I hope not, because you may never get there. Trust me, when you have children, you will make the time to do both. If you set bigger goals, ones that are important to you and the world, you will have to let go of the smaller things that are holding you back.

What things are you trying to balance? Can you picture them on a teeter-totter? Are you doing well at balance, or do you need help in this area? Skills that helped me have been time management, organization, getting clear on my goals, and learning to ask for help when I need it. Balance is not something that you achieve and then forget it. It is something that must be maintained every day. When something changes in your life, you will need to reassess and re-balance, just like my new goals have made me change how I am doing things.

Kids have the same needs as adults when it comes to balance. They have to balance school, homework, friends, sports, hobbies, chores, etc. They aren't always going to get that balance right. They will need you to help guide them. They will see what you do and learn from it. If you spend all your time working and don't play with them, they will learn how to do that. If you spend all your time playing and don't work, they will learn that, too. Show them the balance they will need in their lives. Don't hide work from them because they are kids, and don't pretend you don't have kids when you go to work. These are all important parts of your life, and they should be balanced and integrated whenever you can.

On the day my kids and I were trying to balance on a

teeter-totter, my mom happened to be here. She was visiting us from Kansas, where she lives. It was one of the couple times a year that she gets to visit us. We had all gone to the park. After playing on the teeter-totter with my kids (and trying multiple ways to balance on it), Deven and Ethan got bored and ran off toward the swings. Then my mom sat down on one side of the seesaw while I was on the other. We had a great conversation while we played. The kids saw us and rushed back, thinking how funny it was that Grandma was playing on the teeter-totter with Mom. However, I told them how it was easier for Grandma and me because we were pretty much the same size, so balancing didn't take a lot of work. They agreed with that and thought it was great that she was playing with us. Then they both climbed onto different parts of the teeter-totter, and we had to figure out how to balance all over again. We all had a great time that day, and my kids got an easy lesson in balance.

LILA'S CHAPTER OUTLINE

- Choose partners, in business and family, who have different strengths than you.
- Big picture thinkers frequently get bored with the day-to-day running of a business.
- People who run a business frequently focus on the day-to-day and miss the big picture.
- Don't choose between two important parts of your life. You need both! Build a team and you will have enough time for everything that is important to you.

- Create a system.

- If you cannot find balance, don't try harder or work more on a way that you have proven doesn't work. Imagine and create a completely different way to do things.

CHAPTER 3

Give Them Motivation

ERIC'S EXPERIENCES

How do you get your kids to do something? The only experience I had was being a platoon sergeant. Taking care of my platoon in some ways was like taking care of a family. You have to keep them working as a team. There are always times when one is excelling, and another is failing. I frequently think back to the NCO Creed. "I will be fair and impartial when recommending both rewards and punishments." Others would say use the stick and the carrot. That is true. But I find that providing the correct motivation usually works the best.

Even when people thought that the kids were too young to understand, I showed them what their choices could lead to. I taught them that every decision and action leads to a different outcome or consequence. Some of these things are good for you. Others are not. The decisions you make, and the actions you take create every aspect of your life. If you want a different outcome start making different decisions. This may be why the main lesson in Deven's first book "*If I Can Do It So Can You*" is be creative and take action.

In every aspect of life, the Army, Business and family, people will work much harder if it is their idea. I can ask any of you to do something for me and some of you will do it. But if YOU decide that something needs done, you will move mountains to make it happen. One caveat here, people frequently do more for others than themselves. So to properly motivate someone you must help them see that it is their idea and then let them know how much it will help you or the rest of the world. It is a strange balance, but it works.

How do you motivate a child? The same way you motivate everyone else. Find out what they want. Show them a way to get it. Get out of their way. It is actually easier with younger individuals. Adults have much more baggage. I hosted an investor meeting last night. There were people just getting started who had never done a deal. Others had been in business for longer than I had. Some were very successful, and others were struggling. All of us, including me, have excuses. We all have some idea we created that is holding us back. It is so much easier to see these issues in others than to admit them to yourself.

One of our new investors told me over and over, "But, it's so hard." Change is always hard. You have to get out of your comfort zone. You always hear "Think outside of the box." Personally, I like Bill Cook's version much better. "What Box?" First you have to realize that you are the only one who can create a box for yourself. Then you can get out of it. If it is your wife or husband's fault, then you are giving her or him control of your life. If it is your parent's fault, then you are choosing to live in their shadow. Others blame it on their race or gender... Some people can't get rich because they are so poor. Let me ask you, has any poor person ever become rich? Has anyone of your gender, race, religion…fill in any class that you fit in, ever achieved what you want to achieve? If they could do it, then so can you. Quit giving away your power, and take charge of your life!

Everyone has a different motivation. I have met people who couldn't take a risk because they had to provide for their children. I decided I had to make it in life so I Could provide for my children. I have friends whose wives or husbands won't "Let" them invest. In a marriage you don't both have to be involved, but most marriages work out better when you discuss things. One of my first mentors has a deal with his wife. He never brings work home. Tenants don't get the home phone number or come to the house. If the story is true, she told him he could "Play" with this real estate thing until she had to start paying the bills. Then he would have to get a real job. That was around 50 years ago and he has never gotten that "Real" job.

When it comes to your team, your spouse is your most important partner. A couple years after we started buying real estate, a new couple went to dinner with us. I was honored and a little surprised that they thought we were one of the three most successful couples in the room. They grouped us with my mentor and another couple that had been in business for decades. They asked a very good question that I had never thought of. How do you handle this in your marriage? You heard my first mentor's response: "I do everything and never bother my wife with the details. As long as money comes in, she is happy."

The next very successful couple said that no matter who finds the deal, they ALWAYS go home and talk about it that night. After they both agree and sleep on it, they don't hesitate. They take action the next morning together. Then, the new couple asked me what we do. I said, "If I find a good deal, I just buy it. I normally tell Lila when I get home what I had bought." They said, "So you are like your first mentor. You do everything and don't tell your wife." About that time Lila chimed in, "Not really. If I find a deal, I just buy it and tell Eric when I get home that night."

We have decided that we are equal in everything. If she needs my help, she calls me like any other member of the team that she may need. If I need her, I call her. This works for us. I do not think that any of these ways are better than the other. There are definitely no genders or races that are better at business than others. But every individual is better than someone else at something. Find out what those strengths are. Hire people that have what you are missing. Maybe we just got lucky, but it seems that Lila's greatest strengths are all of my weaknesses. If you find a spouse or partner like this, then working as equal partners will work great. If you and your partner have all of the same personality traits, you need to hire people that fill in what you are lacking.

There have been many different people who have sat at our front desk. My wife thought that I didn't like a couple of them. I had to correct her. Just because they are nothing like me does not mean that I do not like them. I reminded her of a couple receptionists that were just like me. It completely changed the dynamics of the company and the tenants that we were attracting. Every business and family needs this diverse dynamic. I know the receptionist we have now is about my polar opposite. And I can't thank her enough. She may be the very best person that has ever sat in that chair. She is the one that can most clearly see the mistakes I am making because she looks at things from a different angle than I. I hope all of you can find a spouse, business partner or employee that compliments you. One who rounds out everything that you are missing. That is how we balance our businesses.

Once you have this balance, you have to realize that you cannot motivate these different archetypes the same way that you want to be motivated. You have to find out what they want. You have to find out what drives them. Some people will do more for extra money. Others want recognition. The world is full of people who want power. And there are others that would do anything to avoid any responsibility. It doesn't matter how they are motivated. What matters is that you find out how to reward them the way they want to be rewarded. Most people will show you what makes them happy if you just pay attention.

I have found that if I do something to avoid a conse-quence, I may succeed, but I never feel good about my success. If I push myself to the breaking point to achieve a goal that I set, I feel an immense amount of accomplishment. It makes me want to keep doing more. Money that you earn or create to avoid fear, pain or any negative emotion will not bring you happiness. At best, it will only diminish the negative. Money created by helping others will bring happiness and joy to both others and to you. This is true for most people. Do all you can to let your family and staff work towards a positive goal. A goal that they have helped to choose and believe in. When people choose what way to go, and know that they are helping their team, they will have way more self-motivation than anything I could ever hope to give them. As for our children, if we react that way, why would children be any different?

ERIC'S CHAPTER OUTLINE

- The decisions you make, and the actions you take create every aspect of your life. If you want a different outcome start making different decisions.
- Don't let excuses hold you back.
- Your spouse's / family's support can motivate you more than anything.
- Hire people who have the traits that you are missing.
- Reward people in ways that they want to be rewarded.
- Work towards positive goals that the team chooses.

- Do not work to avoid pain or get away from bad things.

- Kids are motivated the same way we are. They just have different goals.

LILA'S LESSONS

Learning to hire and manage a team of people taught me a lot about motivation. In the beginning, I thought money was the main motivation for people working. However, over the years, I have learned that it isn't the money in and of itself that was important; it was what the money would buy. Some needed the funds to fix a car, pay for their child's college, or buy their own home. Others needed to get a crucial surgery for a family member. The bigger their "why" for needing the money, the more they wanted to work to get it.

However, I also learned that money is not enough to keep them at a job. They can get money by working at a lot of different places. In addition to the paycheck, they are looking for some sort of fulfillment. Some want to belong to a group that they feel is like a second family. Others want to help people and believe they are making a difference in someone else's life. Many others are looking for achievement in being able to get amazing results and be proud of their accomplishments. While they do want financial rewards for their work, these other, deeper items are just as important to them, even if they don't realize it consciously themselves. I had to learn this the hard way. Even when I was paying as much or more than other companies around me, if I didn't create the right working environment or have a clear communication of our mission, people didn't stay long.

There was a woman that processed our rental applications that gave me one of my first lessons in how to retain a good team member. We paid slightly more per hour than our competitors, and this helped her financial situation. She made a comment to me in the January after she started that, for the first time, she had been able to both pay her rent and buy Christmas presents for her kids without worrying about where she would get the funds. She also had a much deeper need. At the time we hired her, she asked for and got permission to leave a little before 3 pm to get her kids off the bus and settled at home. Then, she would come back and finish her work for the day if there was more that needed done. She admitted that without that freedom to take care of her kids, she would not have stayed for many years like she did. After meeting her financial needs and her deeper desire to be there for her children, she was motivated to do her job well and stay longer.

Now, I have much better retention because I understand that people need money for certain things but that they want something else also. If I can find out what my team wants and help them get it, they will help me keep the business running smoothly, even if I am not at the office while they are working. This is a good exchange of value on both sides.

Finding out what the people I'm interviewing really want is not easy. Adults are not good at telling you WHAT they want. When I interview people, they will sometimes tell me their financial needs, but they usually do not have a clear vision of their deeper aspirations. I ask what they want in one way; then I ask in a different way. I may try to rephrase what I am hearing from them so they can expound on a certain idea. It would be much easier if adults had clarity on what they really want. Once I do discover their deeper goals, they can usually tell me why it is so important to them.

Kids, on the other hand, seem to know exactly WHAT they want. They are not always good at telling you WHY they want (or don't want) something. This makes it much more difficult for adults to determine their deeper motivation. However, if you want to determine this motivation, you can sometimes ask a lot of questions to figure it out, just like I have to do with adults I interview.

Many investors spend many years building a real estate empire, hoping to pass along their properties to their children. Then, they realize that their kids want nothing to do with these properties. This can be disappointing to the investor, who worked hard to build their real estate portfolio. I frequently get asked "How did you make your kids do this?" The answer: we didn't make them do anything. They watched what we did. They wanted things, like new toys, vacations, or just time with Mom and Dad. Then they realized having their own investments could give these things to them.

Sometimes, the problem parents have is how they communicate with their children about their investments, just like I had done poorly in communicating and explaining our business mission to my team members in the beginning. For example, many real estate investors are very hands-on with their properties. They spend many hours fixing properties, collecting rents, and dealing with problems. What their kids see is that the parent is gone for many hours, comes home tired and cranky, and complains about the tenants, trash, and problems they had to deal with. When that is what the kids see, what could possibly motivate them to want to do the same thing?

My kids have seen the freedom that we have because of our investments. We travel when we want, go where we want, and can stay as long as we choose. If there is something we want to buy, like a new car, we just go buy an investment that makes money, and we let the investment's cashflow pay for the car. What our kids have seen is vastly different than what other investors' children have seen. This has made a huge difference.

Do they understand that any investment can have risk or problems? Yes. Just ask Deven about his first duplex. A nice elderly lady had moved into the unit there, and her grandson had started cooking meth in the attic. Thank goodness the police caught this activity within days of it starting. It was bad enough to have to explain to a seven-year-old what meth was, but it was harder to watch his face when he realized that the building might go away but the private loan and mortgage wouldn't. I knew he understood the risk and problems involved. It was a relief when it all worked out and there was no extensive clean-up needed. But, for a couple of days, my son got a hard and fast lesson on what CAN happen with an investment.

So why didn't this deter him from investing more? He had seen how many properties others had purchased without having this problem. He understood that what happened to him was not a common occurrence. Today, he is very proud of his real estate portfolio.

Deven always had a desire to figure out how things work and teach others about it. I believe that the reason Legos were so fascinating to him is because he wanted to figure out how to put them together to make them the shape of things he wanted them to be. Then, he would teach me why one type of piece was better than another for accomplishing a particular look. In school, he wrote "how-to" papers such as how to cut wood and how to dig a ditch. When he published his first book at eleven and started speaking to groups of people, he was very excited to be able to help and motivate them in the arena of investing and real estate.

Ethan, as a young child, liked a challenge. If someone told him that he couldn't do something, he was very motivated to find a way to get it done. He was always smaller than his brother, but he tried to make up for it by being physically and mentally strong. He is my fearless one. I remember working at my desk at home, and all I heard was, "Hey, Deven, look at my parachute!" I dropped everything onto my desk, including my cell phone, and went running. Ethan, at the age of three, was standing on our spiral staircase with a blanket held up behind him. He was ready to jump. I ran up the stairs to get him. That was the day we had to have a conversation about risk and reward, which was not easy to communicate to a three-year-old. While I understood that being fearless has some advantages, I wanted him to have some balance to know that there is sometimes too much risk and not enough reward. The balance between risk and reward is difficult for some adults. We discussed ways to lower the risk on certain endeavors. I knew if Ethan could master these things and pair it with his fearlessness, it would serve him well.

Today, Ethan still likes a challenge. At Boy Scout camp this summer, he joined in a hike up Thunderbird Hill. The scouts are encouraged to bring a rock up the hill that is "the size of their scout spirit". Both of my kids brought up rocks that were almost fifty pounds. Deven was smart enough to put his in his hiking pack. Ethan, however, held onto a rock that was the size of his torso. Everyone could see this rock, and person after person told him that he would never make it up the steep hill. Ethan was only more motivated to make it up there. He was very proud to put his rock in the front of the rock pile, where everyone could see what can be accomplished. Deven put his rock on the very top. Neither of my children will avoid a challenge, although

Ethan is definitely very motivated by things that other people believe are impossible.

What motivates your kids? What motivates you? If you can't easily answer these questions, it is worth the effort to figure it out.

LILA'S CHAPTER OUTLINE

- Money is "A" motivator but not "The" motivator.
- To keep good people offer personal and professional fulfillment.
- Don't Make your kids or staff do anything. Give them a reason to Want to do it.
- When you focus on the good, they will see the good.
- Don't hide the bad...be honest.
- You have to find the balance between risks and rewards.
- It is important to find out what motivates people.

CHAPTER 4

Give Them the Choice

ERIC'S EXPERIENCES

When is the last time you ordered food for your child? For that matter, when is the last time that you ordered for your friend or spouse? I never understood why a man would order for a woman. Sure, if my wife leaves the table and the waitress comes, I order what Lila asked me to order. But I never told her what she should want. I have been married for over twenty years and still don't presume to know what she wants every time. I know her favorite dishes at about every restaurant in town. And as soon as I think she will order the same thing as the last ten times we ate there, she gets something different.

When we had kids, I thought the same way. I did not mean to be rude to the waitress. I really believe the saying that "a person that is nice to you and rude to their waitress is not a nice person." And yet that is exactly what she thought I did. It happened one day when we went out for lunch. Actually, we do that almost every day. And this happened many times. The waitress would come up and ask, "what does your kid want?" Then I said, "How could I know? Ask him."

It was explained to me that some parents are offended if a waitress, or other stranger, talks directly to their children.

Another lunch companion, on another day, told me that only the parents know what the kids are allowed to have. Other excuses for this behavior were: "kids take too long", "it is easier" and even some version of "because that is how it is done." First, I realized how my quick, honest response came out more rudely than I intended and worked to say it in a much nicer way.

What my companions said at these meals, which were really intended as lessons for me by other parents, were: "Some parents are offended" I heard…they are insecure. "They take too long" I heard…it is better to be fast than get what you want. "It is easier"…training my child to make their own choices is not worth my effort. "Because that is how it is done"…because I said so! What I learned in these situations was they really have no idea; they just blindly follow the norm so they could blame someone else when they failed. I am sure that these companions of mine thought they were letting me in on a secret that I should have already figured out. I didn't learn that. I just kept making my two-year-old point at the picture of the food he wanted. Now he makes decisions that have improved his life and the lives of everyone around him.

There is another saying I never use, "Because I said so!" I just went to a conference with a great investor and speaker. His father was a general. He had all kinds of great information. He has done this for decades longer than I. He, and his students, are incredibly successful. He taught that, with kids, there are times that the only reason you need is "Because I said." As great as he is, I disagree with that statement. While there might be emergencies like "get off of the runway RIGHT NOW!", there is always time to explain after the emergency ends what the problem is. In this instance you could tell the child, "I know if that plane hit you, it would be the pilot's fault. You would be right, but you would still be dead." (Yes, that really is the law.)

If I, or anyone else, ever tells you to act without thinking, you better question us more than ever before. Blindly following orders does not work in the Army, in business or in raising children. Can you get it to work? Sure, for a while. Until someday there are too many unanswered questions. That is when your troops/staff/kids rebel. They may quit. They may leave. They may even lead a mutiny or strike against you. If you do everything you can to explain, so they understand WHY they are doing something, you can get exponentially better results. With my staff I give them the system. Whenever I can I allow them to put their own twist on it. I create the solid foundation and they build on top of it with the materials that they have.

No great business makes it without a great foundation. Kids usually don't turn out well if they grow up without discipline and rules. I just think that they should understand why those rules exist. If we, the parents, cannot explain why we have a rule, then we should question if that rule is really necessary. If we are not willing to explain why, then we should ask ourselves what is more important than giving our kids all the information. If things need to be kept in the dark, they generally turn out to be bad ideas and rules.

If you give orders to your soldiers or deadlines to your contractors, the directions may be followed, and deadlines may be met. If you do this too many times, it may start to cause tension between you and them. But, if the electrician understands that you picked Friday the twenty-ninth as his deadline for finishing the rough electrical because he said he could have it done by that Friday, it may be done. If the electrician also understands that the drywaller is starting the following Monday, he may work over the weekend to finish even if he had an unexpected problem that made the job take a few days longer. When you just tell them it has to be done Friday there are only two options. It is done or it is not. When you take the time to explain WHY it must be done, they have more incentive to help you achieve your goals.

Give your kids and your staff the solid foundation that they need to be good citizens and workers. Then trust them to make good choices. It is amazing how many creative things that kids come up with. Deven started by ordering his own food as soon as he could talk. He pointed to pictures even before that. A few years later, when he was seven, he had an idea that no one in our company had ever thought of. It was so simple, and so good, he sold it to the company so they could save time and money in the future. He still gets royalties today from that one idea he had at seven years old. What would have happened if I would have told him "Be quiet now, the grown-ups are talking?"

When you tell people the why, and help them to live a balanced life, they are not only happier, they are also more productive. When you help people to clearly define their own goals and show them how your goals are aligned with theirs, they will amaze you at how far and fast they can go. Encourage them to succeed at everything they do. Let them know you care about their work and their personal life. If they don't have a tool, or even gas money, they will not be effective and might not even make it to work. I design bonuses so my contractors get extra money when the job is completed faster. After all, if I can rent a property a week or two earlier, it usually covers most of the bonus. This is the external encouragement some of them need to be more efficient. Once they are encouraged, and they get motivated, you need to give them the choice as to which way to go. Sure, they hit a guardrail every now and then. No, none of them will ever do it exactly like you would. But they may find ways that you never thought of that are even better and more efficient to accomplish a task. Give them the choice and watch what choices they open up for you.

ERIC'S CHAPTER OUTLINE

- Everyone deserves to choose for themselves.
- Do what is right. Not just what is easy or normal.
- Because I said so is NEVER an acceptable reason.

- Anyone who wants your blind obedience is not worth trusting.
- Everything that lasts starts with a solid foundation.
- When people make their own choices, they can get results that you never would have.
- In all of history, not one person that demanded blind obedience turned out to be the good person.

LILA'S LESSONS

Newton said that every action has an equal and opposite reaction. Similarly, my kids have heard that every decision has an outcome—either positive or negative. When they make a choice, sometimes they like the outcome. Other times they do not. The better choices they make, the more they will like the results.

In order for kids to learn to make good decisions, they must be given the opportunity to make their own choices. This can be hard for parents, who don't ever want to see their kids fail or get hurt. However, parents can't just do everything for them, or they will never learn how to think through things for themselves.

There are many opportunities for kids to make choices that will teach the lessons of good decision-making. Having a child order their own food at a restaurant, knowing that they have to eat whatever they order, is a good example. Choosing what speaker they want to listen to at a multi-speaker event, which vehicle they want to travel in (Dad's

Porsche or Mom's SUV), what school subject to work on first thing in the morning, and what clothes they want to wear are just a few examples of choices we gave our kids. Find ways to give your kids these opportunities.

You can have them make choices while they do a particular task. As soon as Deven was steady enough to stand on a chair, one of his household tasks was to take the clean silverware out of the dishwasher and file away the forks and spoons where they go in the drawer. The difference between a fork and spoon was easy. However, he had to pay attention to the big spoons from the little spoons. He had to decide which of these he was looking at to put them in the right area. This helped teach him attention to detail. It also helped him learn where they each go.

Another example of this is having them write their own yearly goals. Every New Year's Eve, we sit down as a family, usually with some friends, and choose what goals we want for the next year. We have had our kids making their own goals since they were old enough to write. They had to choose what they wanted to accomplish in the next year, including events they wanted to attend, where they wanted to travel, what fun things they wanted to do and what investment goals they had. This made them think about what they wanted, as well as what they needed to do to get there. Getting to choose what they wanted to do gave them the motivation to accomplish it.

When you have a team of people working for you, this same lesson applies. Yes, we have a system manual and need certain things done. This system explains the big picture items that need to be completed. It does not tell them exactly how to do everything. Anytime a team member can use their own creativity to accomplish the mission, we encourage them to do so. People are more motivated to accomplish things when they make choices relating to the task they are doing. For example, the people doing showings may need to explain our pet policy. There are 3 main things they need to mention. We do not give them a script that they have to repeat verbatim. We encourage them to explain it in their own words.

One of the choices Deven and Ethan had to make in the last two years was whether they wanted me to continue to create their curriculum for school or if they wanted to try an online curriculum from Ron Paul. When I made the curriculum, they knew that I could add in a lot of topics that they were interested in. However, they really liked Ron Paul and were curious about what it would be like to try school a different way with different teachers. In the end, they chose both. They chose some courses that Eric & I create and others from the Ron Paul online curriculum.

They REALLY enjoyed their online history teacher's way of telling the history stories. I almost yelled at Deven one day because he was laughing so hard that I was certain he was not doing schoolwork. When I asked what he was laughing at, he told me his history teacher. I walked around to look at his screen, and, sure enough, he was laughing at whatever his teacher had said.

Ethan's first science class through www.RonPaulCurriculum.com included building a robot and a radio. It was very hands on, and he had a lot of fun with that. He also enjoyed his history teacher. They both determined that they liked the online curriculum.

The second year was just as good for Deven, but then, we realized Ethan was struggling more to keep up. The reason: this year's classes didn't have as much hands-on learning. We knew in the future, we would use some of the Ron Paul classes, like the history they both enjoy so much. Other classes for Ethan would have to be more hands on. This way, we can make sure he gets the physical learning he needs.

Making decisions and seeing the results is just one more way for kids to understand, if they don't like their results, they need to make better choices. This is a huge lesson that many adults need to learn today. If they don't like the way their life is going, it is because of the decisions they are making. The earlier kids learn their choices lead to their results, the better their life can be.

LILA'S CHAPTER OUTLINE

- Your choices create your outcomes…Both good and bad.

- Every choice you make when you are younger makes it easier to evaluate situations and make more important choices as you get older.

- Set goals for every part of your life.

- People are more motivated when they make their own choices.
- Tell them where to go, not how to get there.
- If you don't like your results, make better choices.

CHAPTER 5

Give Them the Encouragement: Align Your Goals With Theirs

ERIC'S EXPERIENCES

In chapter three we talked about motivation. I see motivation as more of the internal drive. In the Army we taught that false motivation is better than no motivation at all. When my kids were very young and something bad happened, I gave them false motivation. There is no chance of using logic with a crying two-year-old. After determining that they were not seriously hurt, I would yell "Good Job." Or "What a fall. You did a great job landing!" This helped them to forget about a little pain and got them to think about some part of it that was a success. If they were determined to be in a bad mood, I would make them do jumping jacks. Sometimes it was push-ups or sit-ups. When your mind is so wrapped up in your problems, you cannot learn. When your emotions are high, your intelligence is low. To counter this I had them change their physical state. Think about this, if you are sad can you just choose to be happy? Sometimes, but it takes a while and a lot of patience and focus. Patience and focus are not traits anyone has when they are very emotional. Especially a two-year-old.

If you change your physical state, for instance do push-ups, it helps you rapidly change your emotional state. Perhaps they were just confused why they were hurt, and dad clapped or made them jump around. But they always quit crying and then we could talk about what happened.

Years later Deven would get very upset about something. I frequently did not even know what went wrong. By then, he knew to change his physical state. I would find him doing push-ups or Ethan running around the driveway. When they got done, they would clearly think about a problem and generally solve it or ask for our help. Not only does this give them better control of their feelings and emotions, it also makes them more physically fit in the process. If you think that this could work for you when you need to get through a problem, try it. If you also think that there is no way that you are going to do push-ups in your office, or a business negotiation, be creative. They make grippers for hand strength. Some people rotate two balls around in one of their hands. There is a reason we call these things stress relievers. Simply focusing on your physical state allows you to take control of your emotional state much quicker.

Once you have control of your internal motivation, some external encouragement never hurts. When I first started hiring people, I did OK with the guys in the field. Construction workers are a lot more like soldiers. Looking back, I chose the people who had the personality that did better in that environment. Unfortunately, that did not work at all with the women in Lila's office. I learned, over and over, that barking orders like a drill sergeant was not fast and efficient. It scared people and they quit.

I spent many years in an all-male, combat, airborne unit. It wasn't until my last couple months at Ft. Bragg that we got the first female in our unit. What seemed normal to me was not normal in the civilian world. Or even when interacting with the opposite sex. When I looked back at how I learned to lead, I tried to teach Lila the way I did things. I should have seen that it was not even working for me and there was no way she could lead that way. That caused a lot of stress in our business and our lives. At one time I even gave her the military field manual on leadership. (FM 22-100 is still a good book by the way.) I had never seen an effective leader that taught in another way. My role models for leadership were my dad, who was a "Black Hat" (Instructor for Airborne School.) My drill sergeants. And then my platoon sergeant who led the same way as the last two.

After leaving that combat Airborne unit at Ft. Bragg with no females I went to a medical unit in the National Guard. Here there were more females than men. I was an E6 by then. A low to mid-level sergeant. I looked at my leader there and realized that she was as effective and respected as anyone I ever met at Ft. Bragg. And she did it without yelling.

I realized that just because I found one way to lead, teach and inspire it wasn't the only way. It definitely wasn't the best way. It was just a way that fit my teenage personality when surrounded by a bunch of guys that were jumping out of planes, blowing things up and getting shot at. About that time, I met Blair Singer in Orlando. He was one of our teachers in a course that made us better trainers. I bought his course Lead, Teach and Inspire. I also bought all of his other courses. One of them has the dogs barking that Deven loved to imitate when he was just a couple months old. These, and many other classes taught me that it was not that men taught one way and women taught another. It was that what might have worked in war, frequently does not work in business or family.

With a lot of help from some incredible women in my life I started to learn. With an unbelievable amount of tolerance from my wife, I survived this transition. One of the female teachers I had sentenced me to watching "Chick Flicks" for about a month. No more Dirty Dozen. Now I watch Sleepless in Seattle with my wife. Without any question, this was the area in my life that had the least amount of balance. I am still a little bit too militant with my business and family, but everyone that knew me before will tell you how much I have toned it down.

Thankfully this all happened before my children were too old. While I am still learning and growing every day, I had at least started down the right path by the time Deven was born. Knowing how hard it was for me to change, I wanted to make sure I was a much better role model than I had. I am very glad that I learned the lessons from my dad and military leaders that kept me alive. And I want to teach that to my kids. I just also want to teach them that you can be a great leader without being the biggest toughest guy in the room.

In order to do this, I started listening more than ordering. I focused more on what they wanted than what my goal was. Once I found something that they wanted, I aligned their objective with mine. When they are little, it is easy to encourage them with things like "If you want the new Lego set, and I want the lawn mowed, I bet there is a way we can get both..." And when they grow up you can still do the same thing. Lila was paying people for time and results. I looked at the way she had set up the pay scale for her people doing showings. They actually made $5 more if they did not get an application completed. After running her business for a week when she was gone, I changed everything. With one change that aligned her goals with the people who worked for her, she doubled her results. She paid half as much and still got more completed applications turned in. The leasing reps were also happy. The ones that were best at sales made twice as much as they were making before, and the others moved to other non-sales jobs.

Set up a goal. Make sure everyone knows the goal. Make sure that everyone is rewarded when they get to the goal. And you will dramatically improve your results. Almost everyone wants better results. But few people are willing to take the action and risk the pain to get them. Think of one of the hardest things that you have ever learned. We all had to learn to walk. We all failed more times that we could count. We stood up, we fell down. We did it again. We fell on our butts. We banged our heads on the table. We just kept going until we had mastered that terribly hard action of walking. Why would we do this? Because the benefits of walking far outweigh the pain of falling. We also learn to walk because we have not learned that failing is bad yet. Imagine if you had to learn to walk in the traditional school system. If you were not perfect the first time you got a bad grade. If you kept falling you failed. How many of us could have learned that way? Ethan is a perfect example how wanting something so much can make you do things you have never done before.

I used to think that if you tried enough, you learned ways not to do things. Next you learned the correct ways to do things. Then you got better at doing things. Not for Ethan. He showed me that pure determination can overcome physical balance and pain. He loved to go watch Deven in Karate. He was far too young to be in the youngest Little Leaders karate class. So, he would watch from the bench. He would "Kiah" with the students. He would move his hands like them. Then we were all dressed in our gees. I think Lila and I were black belts, or close to it, by then and we were either going to our own class or helping to instruct the kids. Ethan could not talk yet, but he could communicate very well. I told him he was not big enough to go to class yet. He did not like that answer. I told him he at least had to be able to walk before he could be in class. Yes, he was so young he had not walked yet. Sure enough he stood up, held on to the couch and walked. Then when the couch ended, he kept walking towards the door to go to class.

In a couple months he got better at balance—the kind that allows you to stand for more than about ten seconds. He also memorized the motions to the KATA's that we were doing. Somehow, I convinced the sensei to allow him to "Try out" even though he was below the minimum age for class. Seeing that he knew the entire first Kata, he was allowed to start training with the big boys and girls. A year or so later he won a competition for Kata. He was so short that the trophy came up past his waist. This taught me that no matter how small you are, no matter how new you are, or unexperienced you are, if you want it bad enough you can achieve it. I have always used this to show people that they can get everything they want out of life if they have the right motivation. For leaders, you simply need to encourage your family and staff by making your goals align with theirs. Let them tell you what rewards they want and then find a way to give them what they want at the same time you get what you want.

I wish that all our goals were achieved in this amazing and happy way. They are not. Some are physically painful. Some are scary, which Ethan seems to always find a way to demonstrate to me. Ethan has always been a very physical person. He is the one that is always falling and running into things at full speed. When Deven got his first 4-wheeler he went so slow I yelled at him to speed up. I thought he was afraid. I should have seen that he was just smart enough to slowly and gently learn what he could do with this powerful (I think it was 50cc's) vehicle. When Ethan started driving that ATV, I wanted to get him a full set of body armor to go with his helmet.

One time he was going the opposite way down a narrow trail as me. He was at about full speed, which is much faster than is safe on this narrow trail. Rather than slow down he decided he would just go around me through the woods. There was a stump there... Right beside me I watched my child, who was about five, hit a stump. The ATV went up on two front wheels, and he went straight over the handlebars. Thankfully I had him in Karate since he could walk, literally, so he knew how to fall. He jumped up so fast because he thought he would be in trouble and never took the time to feel any pain. At first, I was worried. When I saw him jump and move that fast, I knew he was OK. Neither of us knew what the other was going to do, so I moved faster. Figuring he was physically in one piece, I told him he better roll his ATV over on his own. And next time slow down and watch where he is driving. I thought that the physical actions would keep him busy enough he could learn to slow down rather than take time to feel the pain. I continued down the trail and around the next corner to our camper.

When he got back, very quickly, I found out that Lila had been about a minute behind me and had helped him roll his ATV back over. She was wondering if she had ruined his punishment for driving too fast off the trail. He was happy that mom helped him, and dad wasn't mad. I was just happy that he was in one piece and my wife was not upset that I left our kid alone in the woods with a flipped over 4-wheeler. These are not things that you can plan, nor would most parents want to. But not all lessons are learned in the ways we would choose. I would never intentionally set up a painful lesson, but if you find yourself in the circumstance, you might as well learn from your mistakes.

ERIC'S CHAPTER OUTLINE

- When emotions go up, Intelligence goes down.
- A physical change helps you change your emotions.
- Choose the right type of leadership for the right situation.
- Align their objectives with yours.
- You can't achieve a goal unless everyone knows what goal you are working towards.
- Some lessons are painful, but with the right encouragement they can be positive lessons.

LILA'S LESSONS

Eric and I have very opposite personalities. However, our fundamental beliefs are the same. We don't lead the same, communicate the same, approach a problem the same way, or encourage in quite the same way. I think this has been a great benefit to our kids, as they get to see multiple ways of leading, handling situations, and making decisions. Because the core message has been the same from both parents, it has been very clear for them what we wanted them to learn, even if we approach the lesson differently.

Our kids have the same differences. Deven looks very much like his father, but his personality is very much like mine. Ethan looks a lot more like me, but his personality is very similar to Eric's. When Eric and I were talking about getting married, none of our friends thought we would make it very long because of our difference in personalities. I told Eric that we could either let our differences divide us or we could choose to use them to our advantage, since his strengths were my weaknesses and vice versa. We chose to make it work for us, and it has. We have taught our kids the same thing. If they choose to work together, they will be a spectacular team.

When it came to working with our kids, we knew that, sometimes, Eric had to be the one to handle a situation with Deven because of the difference in personalities, and sometimes I had to work with Ethan. Deven was frequently too reserved and could let fear slow him down. Working with Eric taught him how to handle risk and work despite fear. Ethan, on the other hand, needed my more conservative approach to learn to manage risk since he was more prone to jumping into something without thinking it through first. In other words, we tried to balance our children's own personalities by letting the parent with the opposite perspective communicate with them.

Other times, Eric or I would handle something because it was very similar to a problem that we experienced as a kid and wanted to help them overcome. For example, once, when Deven was very little and we were introducing him to someone new, he tried to hide behind me. I did not accept that behavior. I was too quiet, shy, and unable to handle confrontation as a teenager. I was not going to have my child have the same bad habits as I'd had. So, I did with him the same thing I had done to overcome my fear of people...I put him into acting class. This made him communicate and work with others in a way that was fun and empowering. From that point on, even if he wasn't completely comfortable in front of people, he would make the effort to introduce himself and talk to new people.

This really made a difference at the martial arts studio we were attending. I was sitting on the bleachers between two men. The one on my left found out I was homeschooling and proceeded to admonish me for ruining my children. He was ranting about how they would be completely anti-social, when the guy on my right tapped my knee, pointed to Deven down in front, and asked "Is that your kid running for president?" We were all silent as we looked down at young Deven, who was shaking hands with someone in the front row of the bleachers and saying "Hi, my name is Deven." Then he moved to the next person on the bleachers and introduced himself. He kept going down the line of people, introducing himself to everyone. I looked at the guy who had just been telling me how unsocialized my child would be, but he looked away and didn't say another word to me. The point had been made.

Not all the encouragement my children received was from Eric and me. There were other moments in which everyone from leaders to complete strangers helped to encourage them. I remember when Deven decided that he wanted to work to earn his Ohio Professional Housing Provider Certification. He had to attend a lot of REIA meetings to get all of the credits he needed in the right categories in order to earn this. Some of these credits were hard to find, so he had to research and ask one of us to drive him to different places in Ohio to get these. While he was working on this certification, he walked up to Vena Jones Cox, who runs the National Real Estate Convention, and told her that he was going to be the youngest person to ever get his OPHP Certification. Vena looked at him for a moment and then told him, "Deven, I have no doubt that you will." Many people are too intimidated to even talk to her, but he marched right up to her to tell her this. To have her believe in him meant a lot.

A year or so after that, Vena hosted an event called the Wild, Wonderful Women of Real Estate. All of the speakers were women, including several that Deven really liked to listen to. During one evening of the conference, the women speakers were sitting together at a table in the restaurant. Many of the attendees were also in the room. Deven walked right up to the table of speakers and started talking to his favorite ones. Next thing I knew, they had pulled a chair up from another table and invited him to sit with them. They also bought him a soda. One of the adult attendees that we were talking to made a comment that, "Of course your son would just sit down with them. I'm too intimidated to even talk to them, and he's sitting with them!"

I was not surprised by this. Deven liked and respected these women, and he wanted to thank them for teaching him so much. He had no expectation of being asked to join them nor did he worry about being turned away. He had no fear of talking to a well-known national speaker. The attendee that we were talking to, as well as many adults in the room, had this fear, but most kids don't. Someone has to teach them this fear. Avoiding someone famous that you want to talk to is illogical. What are people afraid of? The worst that could have happened is the women would have asked Deven to leave them alone so they could talk, and privacy is a reasonable request. However, people were so afraid of being rejected that they missed out on possible acceptance. Deven only wanted to talk to these women.

He did not think of it in terms of acceptance and rejection. There is a good lesson for everyone in this.

****

DONNA BAUER - THE NOTEBUYER

Although it was years ago, I remember Deven joining us at the table in the restaurant. Robyn Thompson, Wendy Patton and I (Donna Bauer) were all vying to be "Deven's favorite speaker." As we tried to sway him, he was so tactful to make sure to point out what intrigued him about each of our topics. I was very impressed that at such a young age, Deven was actually able to not only understand, but also articulate, the various facets of real estate that we taught. But then again, it should be no surprise— Deven was always seated right up front in our talks, and he was always mingling with the crowd or hanging out at our table in the bookstore to glean whatever he could from us. Dressed in his sport coat and dress shirt with his lanyard on and his portfolio under his arm, the youngest person in the room was one of the most attentive listeners in the crowd. From the time I first saw him, I thought to myself, "This young man is going to be highly successful."

— **Donna Bauer, The Original Notebuyer**
   www.TheNoteBuyer.com

****

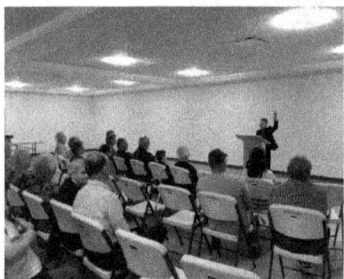

When Deven published his first book at the age of eleven and started talking to large groups of people, everyone told me how impressed they were that he was not afraid to speak in front of people. I asked Deven about this, and he told me that he was afraid but that he did it anyway. It was very rewarding when the audience members told him how much of an impact hearing his story had on them. One guy told him that he had been ready to give up on real estate, but that after hearing Deven speak, he was going to try again and make much better decisions this time. After all, if a kid can do it, so could he!

The more groups Deven spoke to, the easier it became for him to do this. Now, part of him really looks forward to being able to get up and help a large group of people learn the things he has learned. What started as encouragement from Eric and me became encouragement from the people that he spoke to. He also got encouragement from those he was speaking with. He has had some amazing people supporting him in his journey of helping others, including Vena Jones Cox, Bill Cook, Tarl Yarber, Ken McElroy, Mark Victor Hansen, Pace Morby, and many more!

Ethan has never needed much encouragement to talk to people or do something despite fear. I call him my fearless one, not because he doesn't sometimes feel fear, but because he doesn't hesitate to do what he wants to do even if he does feel it. While his brother is speaking at different events, Ethan is the one who will go around introducing himself to everyone and talking to them. When people come up and tell me that they've talked to my son, I have to ask, "Which one?" Because while Deven may have been the speaker in the front of the room, Ethan will have been the one that moved about the rest of room and met a large amount of people. He knows how to "work a room" and ends up being very memorable to those he speaks to.

Ethan has always been a natural communicator. When I was trying to make a "pet video" to use in our property management business to explain our pet rules to tenants, I decided that it would be better to have kids telling them the rules and requirements. If an adult were to tell them rules, they may ignore it. If two cute kids were saying these things, it was more acceptable, so they might remember and be willing to follow these rules. I wrote a script and had Deven and Ethan play the starring roles. Ethan was young enough that he still couldn't say his "L's" correctly. I had to work with Deven somewhat to get the right presentation, but Ethan, although younger, even if he didn't get the words correct, was perfect! He could have been a child movie star with the talent I saw.

This talent of communication combined with his personality has made Ethan a natural to help teach others. He has now taught from stage as well, and he has an easier time at it than Deven did initially. Together, they will be an amazing force for positive change in helping other people learn and gain financial education.

What Deven needed for encouragement growing up was not necessarily the same things Ethan needed. We had to adjust what we did for what each of them needed. Deven has always wanted to learn and then teach others, but he didn't always have the confidence in his communication. We encouraged that confidence. Ethan didn't need that same support but has needed encouragement in other areas. Find out what your kids want and help them learn what they need to get it. If they want it, they will be motivated to get it, and with your help and encouragement, they will learn how to achieve their goals.

LILA'S CHAPTER OUTLINE

- Everyone learns best if they see the lesson from two different points of view.
- At times you need a mentor with your personality and at other times you need the opposite personality to help you overcome obstacles.

- If you don't ask the question, you will never get a yes.

- A less intimidating rule enforcer, like a cute little kid, can say things directly and still sound kind.

- There is no stronger force than a team of people with different personality traits working together.

- We all learn in different ways. Encourage your family and team to learn every way they can.

CHAPTER 6

....

Give Them the Tools: Surround Yourself with the Right People

ERIC'S EXPERIENCE

In the 2001-2002 school year I taught Anatomy, Physiology & Advanced Biology in a local High School. I had graduated with a pre-med degree and then did not go to medical school. After spending most of my life preparing to be a doctor, I realized that I loved medicine. I loved being a medic in the Army. I loved helping patients in the emergency room and in the ambulances I worked in. Then about 3 am in the ER talking to a doctor who I really respected I made the decision to stop now. Civilian medicine was not like in the Army. It was paperwork and rules. These rules were written by the insurance companies, and they were enforced by hospital administrators who didn't have any medical training. There are plenty of issues with military medicine, but the main focus was to save lives. Even before Obamacare (the Affordable Care Act) I was realizing that people with no medical knowledge were dictating what trained and experienced doctors could do to their patients. In the Army we did not have health care. We had injury care. We had disease care. In the real world it seemed like the only care we had was about making money. If we could accidentally fix a broken person too, all the better.

The worst part was that almost all the doctors and nurses

I worked with were fantastic. They were great people who wanted to help their patients. They came to work to find out that they could not order a simple blood test called the Chem 7 one day. Apparently, Medicare would not pay for it anymore. So, we started doing the Chem 6 and then there might have been a Chem 8. Then basically the same test was called the BMP for Basic Metabolic Panel. This was a basic and inexpensive test to see the levels of different chemicals that are in your blood. The "Insurance Companies…" took this tool away from the doctors. The same companies required EKGs on kids with chest pain to CYA (Cover their butts). They were controlling the tools that doctors could use without having the one-on-one personal relationship with the patients.

Somewhere around 3 am one morning in the emergency room, Dr. Shara told me that he loved medicine. He could not imagine doing anything different. And if it was this hard to practice now, he could not imagine what would happen in the next thirty to forty years while I was practicing. That was one of the last pieces I needed to make the decision to look for another career.

I ended up teaching at a private school. I didn't have a teaching certificate. I had never had a class in college on how to teach. My experience was years as an instructor in the Army and I was a skydiving instructor on the weekends. But if a private school needs you, they can get you a temporary certificate. I was already "different" when I showed up. I just went up to the third floor with the rest of the science teachers and everyone left us alone. The one time an administrator came to my room to evaluate me I had the class rolling out a snakeskin that was about 20 feet long. She rolled it across her desk to the next student. I don't think she enjoyed that much. She never came back to my class. Or maybe she thought I was such a great teacher that I never needed checked on again. I did not hold my breath for that evaluation.

These are the things I did in my class. I knew that some people could look at a picture and memorize a muscle. But most learn better by seeing and touching. So, we did a lot of dissection in that class. Almost half of my classes were labs. I wanted to teach the way my students learned. There was a big push to make everyone tuck in their shirts. The fashion for girls then was a shirt that was about 1 inch longer than your waist. There is no way that can ever stay tucked in. I was not about to fight the battle to get the entire female half of the class to buy new shirts. Nor was I going to waste my time telling them to tuck it in. This seemed to take up most of the class time in some other teachers' classes. I told them I did not care about the shirts. Half the time they would want to have a lab coat on anyway. For a bunch of conservative Catholic school students that all wore the same uniforms there were really no issues like we had in high school when I was a student.

The administrators and many other teachers also had a problem with chewing gum in class. There was a long list of rules that did not help me teach. They just helped every student look and act the same. Since no one ever came up to the science floor I enforced rules a little differently. I told them that when they walked downstairs from my class they better tuck in their shirt and look perfect. If they did not, I would get checked on and I may have to start enforcing that rule. I told them I did not care about gum unless we were actively dissecting something. But if any ended up on the bottom of a desk that rule would be enforced. In English they had to sit-down, shut-up and were not allowed to cheat. I told them to get up, find a partner that knew things that they did not know, and work together to learn what I was teaching. I even gave a couple of group tests. I have worked in an operating room, and I assure you that the surgeon doesn't have time to adjust a light. They probably can't find what drawer the tools they need are in. That is why they have a team. Each member knows their job and is efficient. Each member knows exactly where their tools are.

This is what I wanted to teach my students. That they need to form teams. If all you learn is to sit-down, shut-up and memorize you will be perfectly equipped to pass a test tomorrow. Then you will probably forget most of what you memorized by next week or next year. Even if you remember these facts, they have very little correlation with real life. These are tools. They are just not the tools that can help you succeed in life.

The students questioned the dress code. I questioned it also. I asked myself if it was more important to spend 40 minutes teaching teenagers how to dress or to teach them the subject they came to my class to learn. I decided that there were plenty of teachers on the lower two floors that tell them how to wear their shirts. I had more important information to give to them.

Have you ever blindly accepted anything because that is the way it has always been? I do not. I teach my students and my children to question everything. I can never give them all the tools they will need in life. I can teach them to find the tools they need well after I am gone. That starts with questioning everything. A mother heard me say this over and over at one of my business classes. After class she came up to me. She asked, "you mean except you, right?" She wanted to make sure that I taught my kids to question everything except me. She knew that of course they had to accept everything I said because I said it. I did not even answer her. I asked Deven what I had taught him about this. He said, "Oh no. Dad says question everything, especially him!"

The people who love us the most, frequently want us to be safe more than they want us to be successful. I tell everyone if what I say is not logical or seems incongruent, question me. Either you misunderstood, or I am making decisions that are not getting either of us closer to our goal. Both of these mistakes need to be corrected. We can both learn from it. I can never learn or grow if everyone accepts everything I say.

As parents we need to accept that alone, we are not

enough. As business leaders and owners, we need to accept that we cannot do enough. If we are the smartest person in the room, we need to find a bigger room. I am not saying that we are not good enough in any way. Just that there are people in the world that are better at some things than we are. Most people send their kids to school to learn from teachers. We send them to sports to learn from coaches. Why do we quit learning from other teachers and coaches? Name one athlete who is at the top of their game who is so good that they don't need a coach. There isn't one. Why do we as parents or entrepreneurs think that we have to know everything and do everything? Is it because we were taught not to cheat in school? Look at any successful business. Name a single one that is growing with only one person running the whole show. All of us need to leverage other people's time if we want to grow. We need to leverage other people's knowledge and experience. This is so much better if your kids and employees learn it directly from your teachers. It is always amazing when I meet a new teacher. As you grow you will find bigger and better teachers. Sometimes I hear these new teachers talk and know that one of my previous teachers must have learned from this person also.

If you want your children and your staff to succeed, don't tell them to be quiet. Encourage them to ask questions. Give them a love of learning. Don't make them hate memorization. Let them learn from your teachers and mentors. If you surround them with incredible people, they will become incredible. If you surround them with complaints, and excuses, they will have plenty of complaints and excuses as to why this or that did not get done.

I spent about two years going to T. Harv Eker's courses. I spent another year learning to be a trainer for his organization. Years later I met Mark Victor Hanson. It is amazing to hear him say things that Harv taught me. Every time I hear one of these lessons that is very familiar, but a little different, I realize that this is where Harv learned it. These are the types of people that I choose to surround myself with. These are the ones that always push me to be better. This is who I want my kids to learn from. Lila and I have done a pretty decent job raising our children. We have taught them many lessons. But their results do not just come from us. There was my mom who helped a lot with English. My dad who taught them to build things in the workshop. And remembering that he is grandpa he also probably let them use power tools when they were way too young. There are countless real estate and business meetings that I have always taken them to. There were teachers in theater and the multiple types of martial arts that they trained in. Their first boy scout leader has become my best friend. His whole family has helped and taught my kids so many things that I could not teach, it is unbelievable.

The whole lesson is you can probably brute force it. You can struggle through on your own like you were taught in high school. Or you can have a much easier life and get much better results by building, and trusting, a team. If you think that this is hard, look at my kids. If you can't get up the nerve to walk up to one of these "experts" or famous people, look at anyone's kids. They have no fear. They have to be taught this fear. If you just let them grow and do not teach them what they cannot do, they will amaze you.

The Wohlwend family with Mark and Crystal Hansen

Just this January our family went to the Rebel Capitalist Live event. We are always sitting in the front row. We get up early and stay very late. We meet as many people as we can. Both kids came up after the one day of classes and said that they were exhausted. They wanted to go to the room for a nap before the cocktail party started that night. I let them know they were on their own for dinner. Mom and I were going out with a few other couples for a steak. As I was leaving the restaurant, I realized that I had missed a call from Deven almost an hour ago. I called him back as I was walking back to the conference area. The party had already started. When Ethan answered his brother's phone, he did not say hello. He said, "Not now, Dad. Mark Victor Hansen is introducing us to Robert Kiyosaki!" Now that is a phrase, I never thought I would hear from my twelve year old. These are the results that kids can get, and you can also, if you leave your fear and reservations at the door. There are a lot of tools that we need. There is plenty of great education out there. But the most important thing we need to grow is the people we know. I am honored to have so many great and successful friends. From world renown speakers and best-selling authors to professional athletes and local scoutmasters. We need them all to make our team better.

In the past six months since my children met Mark at a cocktail party we have talked more and more. Mark's partner called the following week. Since then, the whole family has talked, emailed and texted many times. Our family is becoming good friends with his. His wife, Crystal, is talking to Lila and pushing her to learn and grow. Every time we talk, I learn a little more about why they are so successful. Sure, he does all those other things that we learn in every business seminar. But from what I see, that is not his secret power. It is his network. It is the fact that he thinks so much bigger than everyone around. He doesn't talk about fixing the problems of his city. He talks about fixing the problems of the United States. Then he has five more solutions for world hunger. After twenty minutes on the phone with Mark our whole family sits down talks for hours just to unpack all the incredible gems of information that he has given us. A couple days ago he sent us an email. Mitzi Perdue, yes, the chicken company and many other incredible accomplishments, wrote a fantastic biography about him. It is called *Relentless*. I could never imagine a more perfect title to describe him. Early in the morning, late at night and when he is on vacation, he never stops making this world a better place. I have told my children every night of their lives that I love them, and they should dream about making the world a better place. They learned this. They live this. And I think it led them to the perfect person who can help them get to the next level with this goal. And the level after that...

There is a scene from a movie that I think about when I see people taking advice from their friends and family that have all the same problems that they do. The movie is Good Will Hunting. This poor, uneducated kid with a genius IQ tells his professor that all you academics surround yourselves with these books and they're all the wrong books. The lesson I learned is that you need to read the right books. You need to surround yourself with the right people. If you want to grow or do better at anything, take advice from mentors who are better than you are. Ignore your friends who are in exactly the same place as you. Only these coaches and mentors can give you the tools that you are missing.

ERIC'S CHAPTER OUTLINE

- Teach the way your students learn.
- Don't give stupid orders or enforce unenforceable rules.
- Partner with people who know what you don't.
- Develop a team.
- Focus on your goal.
- Question Everything!
- Leverage other people's knowledge and experience.
- Do not teach them to live in fear.
- When your goal is big enough, others will be drawn into your circle.
- Over the next five years you will become the books you read and the people you spend time with... Choose them wisely.

LILA'S LESSONS

We do not shelter our kids. We want them to be prepared to handle the world. When they wanted to get involved in real estate, we knew they would face challenges that adults did not. They needed more than just the information we were learning from the spectacular speakers and teachers we listened to. That part is important, too, but that would be the easy part when they were going everywhere with us and learning from the same people that we were.

I had seen a lot of "parenting gone wrong". One such

moment my kids got to witness also. We had gone out to eat for lunch and milkshakes. We had been seated, ordered, and were waiting on our food when another mom and her son entered the restaurant. There was a wait to be seated, and while they stood there, her son saw the candy machines by the door. I saw him point them out to her, and she shook her head. He tugged on the bottom of her sleeve and pointed to the machines again. She told him no. Then he proceeded to throw himself on the ground, flail his arms and legs, and scream at the top of his lungs.

Everything in the restaurant seemed to come to a stop as everyone turned to see the source of the noxious noise. I saw the mom frantically digging through her purse and thought, "Don't do it." She pulled out coins and couldn't get them into the machine fast enough. Her son got up, took the candy, and was immediately quiet. The hostess told them their table was ready. As they walked past us, I couldn't help myself. I told her, "You just let him win. What lesson do you think he learned?" She gave me a dirty look and continued walking away.

Had one of my kids tried that, they would have been picked up, brought outside, put back in the car, and told that due to their bad behavior, there would be no fun restaurant today. They could scream in the car all they wanted on the way back home, but I would have made it clear that their behavior was exactly WHY they weren't getting what they wanted.

There is a right way and a wrong way to get what you

want in this world. The tool this mother gave her child was the belief that if he just throws a fit and screams, he can get his way. That is the wrong tool to get what you want in the real world. Would you want to work with someone who conducts himself that way? My children have learned to ask, negotiate, and trade value for value. These are appropriate ways to get what you want out of life. These are tools for success. Too many people choose to do what is easy instead of doing what is right. This mom focused on appeasing her child because it was easy, even if it wasn't what was best for the long-term growth of her son.

This is one reason why it is important to pick good team members when you are building your business. You want people who focus on what is right and not on what is easy. The easy route causes people to take short cuts, cheat the system, or cause long term damage to your company. You need to look for people that believe in doing the right thing, even when it is not easy. Finding these people may mean weeding through many applicants, especially in times when there doesn't seem to be enough people looking for work. It is better to take the time to find the right people than to bring in someone that may disrupt the other good team members you already have. You need to gear your interview questions to determine how these applicants handle different scenarios, so you can gauge how they will handle similar circumstances in your business. I like to give the people I interview a hypothetical dilemma and ask how they would handle it, especially when they do not know what our normal procedure would be. This helps me to determine how they think through a problem as well as if they choose an easy route or one that is more beneficial even if it is not easy.

Deven and Ethan have both learned that their most valuable resource is your relationships with people. This is the most important "tool" in their box. The more they give to other people, the more people want to help them back. When they aren't sure how to find an answer to a problem, they can call someone that may either have an answer or know someone else that might know. That means that you need to treat everyone with respect and help them when you can.

There are many ways to show respect, and one of them is to always be on time. My parents taught me that if you aren't five minutes early, you are late! My kids learned this same lesson from us. Showing respect for the people you are meeting by being on time communicates to them that you value their time and believe in doing what you promise. These characteristics are important tools in life and in business, as they help you build trust and relationships with other people.

We also wanted our kids to have the right mindset. We wanted them to learn that the world is abundant. So many people have failed in business, real estate, and life in general, because they believed that there was somehow a shortage of what they wanted, whether that was money, success, or friends. These people seemed to believe that in order for one person to win, someone else had to lose. How long would others continue to work with these people if that's how they do business? No one wants to lose. We have seen how a decision, deal, or goal could benefit everyone involved, and this is how we do business. We wanted our kids to have an abundance mindset, so that they would focus on creating win-win situations.

Ethan got to practice this by helping a landlord that wanted to retire. Her properties were underwater from a sales standpoint. She owed more than what they were worth. However, the monthly payments were low enough to cashflow. Had she chosen to hang onto them until the mortgages got paid down, she would have been fine. However, she just wanted to retire from her job and her real estate. Ethan bought the properties subject to her existing mortgages. She got to retire worry-free, and Ethan got properties that would cashflow and that came with financing. Both sides won.

We also wanted our kids to learn to finish what they start. Eric has always told the kids "If it's not all done, it's not done at all." Many people start projects or tasks and then quit before they get to the end. Can you imagine if you hired someone to paint a room and they only painted the bottom 5 feet of every wall? Would you be happy with that job? Or would you tell them that they need to finish painting the top of each wall? We did not want our kids to go to the finish line. We wanted them to always go through the finish line. The tools of dedication and perseverance are important to get things accomplished.

We also wanted our kids to be independent. They learned that Mom and Dad only help for so long, so they'd better take an active role in learning to do things themselves. Earlier this year, Deven had funding for a new four-unit building fall apart a little over a week before closing. He'd had a private lender set up, but she had a family emergency and suddenly couldn't finance his deal. While I technically hold a percentage of the company, he did not tell me about this problem right away. He took responsibility and started calling other potential lenders himself. The deal did get financed and closed, but it was a stressful few days for him before the closing. Had we sheltered him or not let him make his own choices before this, he never would have had the mental tools he needed to make it through. If he had not built relationships and treated those people with respect for years, he would not have been able to come up with enough money to close on a 4-unit in less than a week. Perseverance, responsibility, respect, and relationships are just some of the tools that we teach our children and our staff to develop.

LILA'S CHAPTER OUTLINE

- Do what is right, not just what is easy.
- Ask, negotiate, and trade value for value.

- Focus on long term growth rather than immediate gratification.

- Relationships are the most important "Tool" in your toolbox.

- Respect others in every way.

- The universe is abundant...Everyone can win.

- If it's not all done, it's not done at all.

- Perseverance, responsibility, respect, and relationships can fix almost any problem.

CHAPTER 7

....

Home School

LILA'S LESSONS

My first thought the day after Eric agreed to homeschool our kids was "Now what?" I had won my case, but I had no idea where to start. So, I started the way I always do when I feel lost: I did a lot of research. I looked at our state requirements, what forms I would need to tell the school system we were homeschooling and took note of any assessments the kids might need.

Once Deven was born, I knew that I would need some sort of curriculum to use to teach him. I looked at many different kinds for sale, but I wasn't really happy with any of them. They all taught letters, numbers, colors, etc. Not a one of them I looked at had anything about financial education beyond the different coins in our currency. I wanted something more.

After many months of frustrated searching, I decided to create my own curriculum. Other homeschooling parents have told me that was a brave choice. It wasn't brave—it was selfish. I wanted exactly what I wanted, and when no one else could deliver that, I knew I could get it if I made my own. It was not as organized or elegant as some that could be purchased, but it had all the regular requirements as well as a business and investing class.

Yes, my kids had that separate class from Preschool on. What does a preschool child learn about business and investing? They learn that money is a tool for trade. They learn the names of the coins in our currency. They learn about different terms such as the words "business" and "investing". They learn the beginnings of marketing and advertising. For example, if I said the word "Subway", Deven would say "Eat fresh". We explained how their marketing worked so that he remembered them and their slogan. None of these concepts are difficult. In future grades, we advanced them into other topics and more intermediate concepts. Once they started investing in real estate, we moved them onto advanced topics, even if they didn't understand them as clearly as we did. They needed a steeper learning curve to accomplish what they wanted to do. Since they were motivated to learn them, they did well with the lessons.

Reading was a big part of their learning. They spend at least a half hour every morning reading. They would always have one fiction book and one non-fiction book ready at all times, so that they had a mixture of different kinds of reading. They might be reading a Robert Kiyosaki or Malcolm Gladwell book one day and a Tuttle Twins "Choose-Your-Consequence" book on another. Sometimes we read books aloud as a family, like the Harry Potter or Rush Revere series.

Many people have asked what a normal homeschool day looked like at our house. I don't think there was a "normal day", especially in the beginning. Everything was a mix of me (or Eric) teaching, them doing homework, projects, CD's, movies, science experiments, and learning from other speakers. One day was not necessarily like the ones before it. There is more of a routine now that the boys are older, as they are busy with so many things. However, we travel more now also, so there is still plenty of variety in our days to prevent boredom.

We relied on their grandmother to teach their English and writing lessons, because she knew these subjects even better than I did. At one point we realized that they weren't learning enough in these subjects. They were only at her house two days per week, and even with me helping the other days, it wasn't consistent enough. Yes, my author sons were terrible at writing at one point. Robert Kiyosaki said he was once terrible at it also, so I guess it's OK if you recover and become a best-selling writer. Best-selling does not mean best writing. Honestly, I think Deven learned more while writing his first book than any English class ever taught him. It was hard work for him, took him many months, and he had to re-write multiple sections as his understanding of English and writing improved.

Have I always created my own curriculum? Yes–up until a couple of years ago when we started integrating an online curriculum. We use this along with the subjects we create the curriculum for. Now it's kind of a mix. Even if you have a curriculum from someone else, you should take advantage of one of the greatest parts of homeschooling— making it more interesting and useful for your kids. Gear lessons, or how you explain something, to a topic that they are interested in. At one point, Deven looked at me and said that he didn't think he would ever use Algebra. I told him that I use Algebra frequently. He did not believe me, so his next assignment had questions on how an attorney was billing hours at so much for the first hour and a reduced rate for additional hours. Another problem was solving the cost of carpeting for a house with a similar method. When he got done with the homework, he could finally see how Algebra could be useful in our businesses and real estate.

Would I recommend that other parents create their own curriculum? Not if you can find what you want. Why reinvent the wheel unless it doesn't work for you? I wanted better financial education for my kids, so I designed it. I knew there needed to be a better curriculum available for financial education that parents could pair with other sources, like the Cashflow game by the Rich Dad company. I wrote this for my kids specifically while they were growing up. Now, many people asked me if they can use the curriculum we created. These parents are looking for good options for their own kids to gain financial education. In order to help them, we are making these courses available. These are courses that you can add to any other curriculum. You can even teach them after your kids get home from the traditional school system.

Some parents I talk to aren't sure if they want to homeschool. No one can tell them what they should do. I can only tell them why I made my choice and what my experiences have been like. Homeschooling for me has been amazing! I got to spend days with my children learning, playing, exploring, and trying new things. Now, I believe my relationship with my children is so good because of being able to homeschool. We've learned to work together, play together, and learn together. It has given us a lot in common as well as helped us to understand our differences.

A couple of parents told me that they couldn't be around their children all day, or they would be miserable. That's sad. My children are the joy in my day, even at times when I have caught them not completing a task they were supposed to do or having too messy of a room! Family life is not always perfect and wonderful, but I cannot remember a time not wanting to be with my kids.

Many parents I talk to want to homeschool but are afraid to do this. If you want something strongly enough, you can figure out how to make it happen. Remember, I had no idea how to start, didn't have anyone to ask for help, and was not sure if I would be any good at the job. What I had, was the desire to do it. That's it. If the WHY is strong enough, the HOW will come also. You just have to be dedicated in learning the how and executing it.

I wasn't a perfect teacher in the beginning. I am still not. I read many books on teaching and how people learn. I watched great teachers instruct and paid as much attention to how they did it as what they were teaching. I went to seminars to get better at this. In the end, I took the scientific approach: create a theory on how to do something and try it out. If it didn't work, make a new theory to test.

If you are concerned that you don't know enough, understand that you don't have to know every answer. If my kids ask me a question I don't know the answer to, I will tell them, "let's find out together." Then, I will show them how I would go about finding that answer, which may mean making a phone call, reading a book, researching online, or going to a seminar. When they grow up, they are going to have to be able to find answers themselves. So it is just as important, or even more important, to teach them how to do this.

If you want to homeschool but are just not sure how to teach a particular topic, you can get help. There are tutors that can be hired to help with some subjects. Homeschool groups help with field trips. Co-ops can be found in which parents cooperate as a group and those good at a certain subject teach that subject. Like everything else in life, some groups are better at certain things or are more organized than others. Choose ones that work best for what you want for your kids. Remember, just like in business, you don't have to do it all on your own. In fact, the people who try to do everything by themselves can never grow. It takes a village to raise a child, just like it takes a team to run a business.

There is a program in which kids in grades 7-12 can go to college classes and get both high school and college credits with one class. It is called College Credit Plus in our area. Deven has taken advantage of this program and has been a college student as well as a high school student, for several years. Home-schooled kids frequently do not get allocated as many hours as public schooled kids, but it is still a program worth looking into if you think it may help your child learn and grow.

One of the challenges we had was that both of our children learned differently. What worked when I taught Deven did not work when I tried it with Ethan. Even though I used a similar syllabus, the method of teaching had to be unique. While it was a challenge and could be frustrating, it was also exciting and rewarding. Now I look back on some of those times with a smile. I can still picture Ethan sitting on the edge of the couch next to me, literally bouncing up and down with a letter block in his hand, trying to read a page from Dick and Jane. At the time, I didn't know if he would ever learn to read. Now, I smile at that picture and how far he has come. In the end, it is the challenges we win that stick with us, not the easy times. I am happy for all those challenging memories!

People frequently ask me if my kids do anything for fun. Many seem to assume that they must work all the time, but that's not true. Their activities are varied, but have included over the years: camping, riding four-wheelers, swimming, fishing, archery, gymnastics (Ethan), acting class (Deven), playing basketball, mini-golf, watching plays in a theatre, watching movies, playing Cashflow, playing games with friends (that list is too long to put here but includes playing multiple sports), creating movie shorts, spending time at hands-on science museums, playing Minecraft, and exploring other computer experiences (like 3-D drawings, writing programs, etc.). I am certain I am missing a lot of things in that list, but those were the first things that came to mind. This does not include any of the traveling and adventures we had doing things like going to Jamestown and learning about the first settlement, going to Vegas and enjoying the architecture and magic shows, zip-lining, go-kart racing, and boogie-boarding in the waves of the ocean to name a few. No matter where we go, there is always something to do and explore. Do they work hard? Yes, but they play hard also.

Eric was a much better teacher than I, and it wasn't because he spent a year teaching in a high school. I believe it started with the teacher who helped him learn to read. Once he understood his own learning, he had insight into the learning of others. I learned more from him on this than probably anyone else. He was a great partner to have for homeschooling, even though there were topics he did not want to teach. He, like Mike Maloney, has a talent for taking a complex subject and breaking it down so anyone can understand it. He helped a lot with teaching math, science, and business and investing. Even in topics I normally teach, when the kids get stuck or the topic is more complicated, Eric helps to break it down for them to understand. Sometimes, just hearing it in a different way is enough. It doesn't matter if you are teaching kids or running a large business, it is very beneficial to have someone with a different personality and perspective helping you!

People tell us they are amazed with our results when they meet our children. However, I believe kids are born with the ability to learn more than we give them credit for. Every child learns at their own pace, and some children need to learn in a different way than others. I think our current school system is outdated in addressing things like how kids learn. They also do not teach real financial education. If there is any financial education it is how to save and budget, not how to start a business or how to invest. Some parents and teachers have tried to reform the current system, but the school system changes very slowly. I think we need a new, better system that will make the old one obsolete. I also believe that Homeschooling can be the bridge in between if not a long-term solution to these problems.

Do you want to homeschool your child? Are you open to improving yourself while you help them learn? No one can tell you what you should do when it comes to the decision of homeschooling, but I can tell you that I am very happy that we made that choice and stuck with it.

I want to see more kids learning about business and investing. I want them to see that there are many options for them in this world besides just getting a job. I would like to see kids learning in ways that they find interesting and ways that help them to understand the lesson, no matter how they learn best. I truly believe that every kid has the ability to learn more at an earlier age than most adults would believe possible. Unfortunately, the traditional school system is more concerned with uniformity than it is with helping students excel. As parents, teachers, and business leaders we need to figure out the best way to teach and communicate to our children, students and staff that they can do great things. There is no age limit on excellence. No one knows a child better than an involved parent, so who better to help guide them to independence and understanding?

I believe the more kids that learn financial education, the more they will be prepared to not only have a better life themselves but also to better the lives of those around them. The next generation could be the one to take a giant leap forward toward making this world a better place. It is our duty to prepare them to do this!

LILA'S CHAPTER OUTLINE

- There are many homeschooling curriculums available.
- You can create any classes you want to add to these.
- We created business and investing courses.
- There are no "Normal" days for home school. Do it however it works for you.
- Teach what your students are interested in.
- You can do anything if you want it bad enough...If the Why is big enough the How will present itself.

- No one knows everything they need to, but these answers are easy enough to find.

- Tutors, homeschool groups, co-ops, seminars, mentors, family, and friends are all there to help you teach.

- The flexibility in your schedule gives you more time for fun and integrates play time with learning.

- Teach everything you can at the easiest level to understand.

- Everyone has abilities far beyond our understanding. Don't hold them back.

- Teach the way they learn. Not everyone is the same.

- Teaching them helps you grow and strengthens your family bonds.

- We must teach the next generation the financial literacy that the traditional system does not.

ERIC'S EXPERIENCES

I had never heard of or considered that we may need a curriculum. I never imagined that there were places that you could buy something like that. I just figured that we are intelligent and successful. I know math and science and can teach. My mom was an English teacher. Lila can write, was a good student and can research anything. If there was something we were missing, like learning a foreign language, we would just find someone who knew how to teach that. I put the intention out there and now two of the people in my weekly mentoring group are Spanish Teachers.

Like Lila, I wanted to teach what I thought my kids would need to survive in the real world. I did not want them to memorize the periodic table. I wanted them to understand that the elements on the far right are not reactive with other elements. I wanted them to know that the first column is the most reactive, but in the opposite way as the second to last column. Shooting was one of the things that my dad taught me and I wanted to teach my kids to shoot a bow, rifle, pistol...anything that was useful or fun at the time. I own multiple businesses and have never had a business or accounting class in my life. Going to school for this may have helped me. But I also frequently think that it may have taught me that what I have accomplished was impossible. I wanted to teach my kids that nothing was impossible.

I wanted to teach my kids business in a way that was fun. I wanted them to see that it is possible to get unbelievable results. I knew if I could teach them to see that I was the only one holding me back, they could surpass me. I don't want them to increase my businesses by 10%. I want them to surpass me by so much that they look back and say, well dad had a good start. It was not enough to teach them to run and grow a business. They needed to learn to start a business against all odds. I believed that if they could do that, no matter what I may leave to them, no matter what may happen to them, they would always be fine. They could start over from anyplace, against any obstacle and succeed in life.

This is why I knew we had to homeschool. Like everything in my life, I cared more about how we could do this, than on the rules some agency may make up to protect my children from me. That statement is not even fair. I only saw how we could do this and why it was needed. I never even considered that there may be rules that we may need to follow to be able to do it legally. It is a good thing that Lila was there to research and do all the boring paperwork that makes this legal for us.

If you don't think you are qualified to homeschool, I disagree. Ask, does anyone love my kids more than me? Do any of the teachers at a traditional school care about my kids more than I do? Does school really prepare you for life? Does a college degree guarantee you a good job? Did you ever sit in class wondering why you had to memorize something that you would never use? If you still remember that thing you had to memorize, have you ever used it in life?

These questions should show you some of the problems that the commonly accepted theory is creating. The mantra that was drilled into me by my parents and teachers was: Go to school. Get good grades. Get a college degree. Get a good job. Save money. Invest for the long term. Dollar cost average. Retire at sixty-five and live off your savings and 401K.

What I heard was: work 40 hours a week for fifty weeks a year for forty years of your life. Then you can retire on half as much as you made while you were working. At the same time, you will have twice as much time to spend that money. When I was in grade school my dad told me to put money in the bank at around three percent interest. He did a great job explaining compound interest. I really got it. I saved money. Then I heard about inflation. I asked what it was. He explained it and told me it was about 8% at the time. It seemed to me like compound interest could work the other way. I asked if I put $100 in the bank at 3% interest, and inflation rate 8% of what I could buy, didn't I lose $5 every year? I bought a new bike and spent a lot on aquariums that year before the prices went up.

If I could figure this out when I was about eleven, I could not understand why these educated adults who cared for me still told me to save money. These same adults use to say that "Youth is wasted on the young." I chose to do things my way based on the results I saw in life. Not what my teachers and parents told me to believe. By seeing things the way they are, not how I wish they were or want them to be, I became financially free and retired for the first time when I was only thirty years old. If you think that youth is wasted on the young you should look at the other side of that coin. I say, "Retirement is wasted on the old." Join me on this side. Life is much more exciting! Now, I am teaching my kids to see the world from a different point of view. I do not teach them to blindly follow me, I teach them to question all their assumptions. Especially what the people who love them the most tell them. If they do this, they will not choose the path less traveled. They will create a path in life that none of us will ever see.

If you think that you are not "Smart" enough to teach your kids, think again. Even educated people tell me "Well I could handle the math and science, but I could never do English…" So, find someone who can do what you can't or do not want to do. That is what home school groups are for! I would not try to buy real estate without networking with other investors at REIA meetings. If you want to buy retail, call a Realtor. If you want a deal, network. Look outside of the traditional system. If you want your children to memorize things that they will probably never use, send them to school. If you want an easier path, do what everyone else does. If you want a deal, or to get extraordinary results, find or create a different system. I recommend a home school conference or group. It is much faster than recreating the entire wheel.

Do you know that we learn almost everything we need to know by fourth grade? Sure, an engineer is much better at math than my twelve-year-old who is learning Algebra. An English teacher can probably tell you what the ploo perfect tense is. I just looked it up to see how to spell "Ploo" and I don't even understand the definition of that tense. As Kiyosaki says, I am a best-selling author. Not a best-writing author. Do you learn all these things that you will probably never need just so you are well rounded? Most people forget most of what they learned after fourth grade unless they actually use it in their life. Do you remember differential equations, the parts of the periodic table and how to conjugate a verb? There is a reason that kids can beat educated adults on *Are You Smarter Than a 5th Grader?*

Don't worry about what you don't know. It is not important. Your kids will guide themselves more than you can believe. If they get interested in something they will teach you. I grew up with computers...sort of. The personal computer was just entering our homes when I was in grade school. I learned to program in Basic. The first "Computer Class" was taught in my school when I was in fifth grade. My friends and I knew much more about computers than most of our teachers by then. It was new to them. They did not have a class for it. They did not understand it. They kept trying to use linear thinking about a subject they understood to explain computers to us. We just turned it on and started playing. We made mistakes. We messed everything up. Eventually we learned. Then, in many of my computer classes all the way through high school the teachers called me upfront to teach. Last week I had Deven show me how to put words on my Instagram videos. I never taught him that. He just figured it out. Then, since I acknowledged that he was much better than me, he took the time to teach me what he knew.

The point is no one knows everything. We don't even know everything we need to live. I need someone to fix my car. Could I learn more about mechanics? Sure, but I don't like to do that. I have friends that love to work on cars. I hate it. Why should I work on my weaknesses when other people love to do those things. I have a deal with my airplane mechanic. He keeps my plane in the air, and I keep getting him great real estate deals. That is what I love to do and am good at. When your kids ask about something, teach it to them. When they have interest in something, make it the next class. If you do not know anything about it tell them to research it or find someone who understands that subject. You do not need to know everything. You just need to know who does. Like Henry Ford, you just need to know who to call.

Why do parents choose to pull their kids out of a school system and then try to recreate the same system at home? I had that same problem. I did not believe that you had to start at 8 am. I did not believe that you needed exactly forty-three minutes of history a day. But I did try to approximate the system of the traditional schools. Then I met Rhea Perry. I don't know how many times I heard her tell parents to quit doing that, but it finally sunk in.

I didn't even know that there were homeschool conferences. Then a mutual friend, Larry Goins, told me that I needed to meet Rhea. A few weeks later the whole family went to our first home school conference ever. We heard a speaker or two. They were not polished. They seemed to barely be getting by. They seemed to have good pieces of information, but they did not transfer that info to the audience well. I had been expecting some of the greatest speakers on earth, like the ones I worked with and saw at business conferences. Here we had stay-at-home moms (there were basically no dads there) whose last audience was their seven children. Yes, they all seemed to have huge families. Then came Rhea. She was not shy, and she was definitely not reserved. After talking to her in her booth for a few minutes she stole my children. I had another flashback to Peak Potentials. Next thing I know we are almost running to the room she was speaking in. She hands my kids a microphone and they start talking. This was their first time onstage. She and the audience were amazed at the results these kids had achieved. She invited us back to her booth and told us that we were the family that she had always wanted to meet. We ended up having dinner with Rhea and a couple of her other friends that evening. Now we have all become very good friends. "Mama Rhea" tells this story a little differently than I remember it, so I'll let her fill in her two cents.

****

RHEA PERRY-EDUCATING FOR SUCCESS

When I first heard Deven's and Ethan's stories, I realized that these two amazing young men had already done the things I have been encouraging home schoolers to do for over twenty years.

So when I asked Eric if he would give me permission to introduce his two sons during my workshop on How to Homeschool Teens for Home Business as an example of how parents could educate young people in what I call

Real Education, he promptly turned to the boys and said, "Have you got your elevator speech ready"?

I said, "They have elevator speeches"?

Eric said, "Of course they do. They are businessmen and have been attending business meetings all their lives. Of course they have an elevator speech."

So, we went to the workshop room where about a hundred or so parents were settling in for one more workshop. I did the presentation as I've been doing for over 10 years and when I got near the end, I said, "Would you like to meet real live examples of what you can do with your children once you've lit their fires and learned to educate them according to their interests?"

Of course, the audience gave their permission. I asked Deven and Ethan to join me on the stage. Deven was wearing a suit, which only vendors do at homeschool conventions, and looked very professional. I handed the mic to Deven and said, "Would you please introduce yourself"?

And he did, just like a pro! He didn't sound nervous; he didn't stumble over his words and he didn't shy away from the opportunity.

He basically said, "Hi, my name is Deven Wohlwend, and I have been investing in real estate since I was seven years old. I actually started with Legos when I was five. I'm now twelve years old and own twenty-seven units. I've also written a book that is available for sale on Amazon called *If I Can Do It So Can You*. I'll be here all weekend so if I can help you, just stop by Miss Rhea's booth. Thank you."

When he finished, the audience gave him a hearty round of applause. Then I handed the mic to Ethan.

He said, "My name is Ethan Wohlwend and I'm nine years old. I've been investing in real estate since I was seven and I actually own one more house than he has. I own twenty-eight units."

Everyone laughed and clapped, and I thanked them for their assistance in the workshop.

From that day on, I have been in love with this family who has been on the same track as my family and is doing the same types of things that we did with my seven children on our farm, the Backside of Nowhere in Southern Tennessee for twenty-nine years.

I even asked The Old Schoolhouse Magazine if they would like me to write an article on the Wohlwend family, which they agreed would be wonderful. You can read it in the Winter 2019-2020 issue.

During the interview, I learned that Eric and Lila included his parents in their children's education by letting them spend a day or two every week with Eric's mom who had taught writing, shorthand and typing in a business college and who encouraged them to study grammar. Every two weeks, they spent a day with Eric's dad, a retired dentist, who enjoyed working with them in his woodworking shop and caring for a variety of birds such as pheasants, quail and even some peacocks.

What amazing memories both the boys and their grandparents will have forever of all that time they spent sowing into each other's lives! Multi-generational education is incredibly valuable when done right and what better English teacher to have than your grandmother! Plus, the weekly day off was probably an extra benefit for Lila and Eric.

Now that we've gotten to know each other, the Wohlwend family has become a valuable part of our online community of entrepreneurs at Educating for Success. It's a small tribe of families throughout the country who are educating themselves for home business instead of having a job working for someone else. It's so fun to have them with us because I never know what they'll be into next!

At one cryptocurrency conference a few of my friends attended in faraway Cincinnati, Ohio, our gang of families came in and sat down on the far side of the room. Being an OCD event planner, I looked around to see if there was anyone there I actually knew, when I saw Eric sitting in the front row. I texted him and said, "Look right." He did and we all waved. By the end of that event, several other attendees had joined our little band and the conference was even more fun because of our new friends. It's called networking. Some people teach students not to speak to strangers. Wise homeschooling parents teach their children how to introduce themselves to millionaires and experts in their fields to build win/win relationships that may lead to further projects.

You never know who you're going to meet when you attend a live conference so that's just one reason why I not only encourage families to take their children to educational conferences of all kinds, but for twenty years, we hosted the only home business conference of its kind for homeschooling families. At our last 3-day conference in 2021 in Florence, Alabama, guess who our four featured speakers were?

Eric, Lila, Deven and Ethan Wohlwend.

You know they were a hit!

— **Rhea Perry**

www.EducatingForSuccess.net

****

One of the most important lessons I learned from Rhea was that you do not need so much structure in the traditional sense. Her kids had informal classes at the dining room table most mornings but those often got in the way of what she calls Real School, like when they helped their carpenter dad build houses. When I was about thirteen, I added an addition on to our home with my dad. I learned more useful things about plumbing, wiring, roofing, cement, and every aspect of building than all of the things high school taught me that year. When Rhea said we could let our kids stop taking classes and just build things I wondered why I had never thought of that.

The time for learning history is when they ask a question about history. The time to teach trigonometry is when you need the Pythagorean Theorem to see if a wall is square. Let your kids learn by doing the things that they are interested in. They will be way better students and will find ways to teach themselves even if you do not know the answers to their questions. This is a HUGE key. Never try to tell them something that you are not sure of. It is not only OK, but also essential to admit that you do not know everything. Bad schoolteachers need to know everything. What they know is in the answer key in the back of the book. Anything else is "Beyond the Scope of this class." One of the best college professors I ever had, made me come to his office after class. I frequently asked questions that were "Beyond the scope of this course." I hated that answer. All that saying meant to me was the teacher doesn't know and will not admit it or they are too lazy to explain it to me. When I was in a doctorate level class, I was the only undergraduate there. It was Evolutionary Biology, and I asked the professor, Dr. Hoy, a question. He said he would get back to me and kept teaching. After class he asked me to come to his office. When we got there his went through papers on his desk. Finally, he found a note or a card. He gave me the name of another practicing PhD. He said, "I don't know your answer. No one does. But this is the foremost expert in that field today. If anyone can answer it, he can. Here is his number."

Now, that is a teacher that you can respect and admire. Dr. Hoy really worked in his field. He only taught a semester here and there. He not only admitted he did not know something, but he also went out of his way to help me learn the answer I wanted to know. He stands out as one of the two best professors I had in college. You can be just as good, and you do not need to know everything. You just need to admit that you don't know and, when possible, find out who does have the answer. Is that really any different than running a business? Don't we hire the people who have the strengths and knowledge that we don't?

Like I said before, I like to teach whatever comes up. I love the challenge of teaching calculus using only fourth grade math. The part I can't stand is making sure we check all the boxes. These boxes are designed and required by people who have never worked or lived in the real world. All you prove by checking the correct boxes in school is that you are perfectly equipped to be in school. If you get all the best grades from the best schools, you are qualified to grow up and never leave the school system. You can be a college professor. If you are really intelligent and master the system, you may even grow up to be one of the hundreds of PhD economists at the Fed who has never had to make payroll. Then you can help set the price of money and try to control an uncontrollable system with a formula that you know doesn't work. Since you have no outside experience, you may even make remarks like we know our formula is flawed, but we have to keep using it because we don't have another one. It is obvious to these academics that everything has to be controlled by formulas.

I believe the free market works no matter how hard you try to change it. I don't see how checking boxes on a form could possibly improve my children's chances of success. Thankfully we have Lila for the day-to-day activities. She keeps us a little more structured. She also deals with all the government compliance paperwork.

We have always taught the school year from January to December. It only makes sense. We do not need a spring break to plant crops. We do not need to work the farm in the summer. Although the orchard does take some time in the fall... We do not blindly accept societies norms. I have always questioned why things were the way they were. We chose to do things our own way. It was more logical and efficient. I still need a licensed teacher to sign off that my kids are learning at the right level every year. Usually, these teachers are great. They spend a lot of time teaching us during the evaluation about what other resources are there for what my kids are missing.

Then one time we met a new teacher. She decided that we did things the wrong way. It did not match her answer key. She thought my kids were too young to be in the grade they were in. She said, "You can't get any credit for the work that you did before September because that is when the school year starts." She did not care that they had been evaluated in January the year before and had completed the required lessons. She was completely shocked after telling me how awful we were doing that I thanked her, paid her, and asked her to leave. She must have thought that I was one of her students asking for permission. I knew that I could never change her ideas. Those ideas had gotten her this far in life and she was staying there at any cost. I knew that I was at a good place in my life, but I always wanted to grow. I wanted to do more and be better every day. I would never stop questioning authority or accept anything because "That is just the way it is."

Knowing that we would never agree, I thanked her and handed her a check for her time. She was shocked. She said "Well, I won't sign your kids off." I let her know that I would never expect her to lie for me. I would never ask her to go against her beliefs. They just were not my beliefs. I immediately found another teacher who was open to something new. She was a great teacher because she was always ready to learn. She told us that Deven did not know some of the things that they teach in English class, but if he could write a book at ten years old, he definitely passed English that year. Now I find that there are many teachers that are great people. They are knowledgeable. They are caring. They really want what is best for the kids. And their union doesn't support their beliefs. It is a shame that we have so many kids who want to learn. We have class-rooms of teachers who want to teach. We have millions of parents who want the best for their children, and our education system is still so broken. That is why we need this book. That is why we are writing this—to design a system to replace the old one. Many of these great teachers who are stuck in a broken system are seeing this also. Last week I had five high school teachers and one principal who showed up at my weekly mentoring meeting.

Until we replace the current system, we still need to check the boxes. Thankfully, Lila is there to do that. If she did not, my kids would be getting an impromptu course on how to challenge an overreaching government. But that is the subject of a whole other book.

For you dads out there. Don't be sexist. Of course your wife is better at some things than you. But that does not mean that she gets to have all the fun teaching your kids. We have a lot of experience teaching and doing. Our children need both perspectives on life. We need more dads at home schooling conferences. We need to take a more active role in our children's futures. I don't care if you are tired after work. Ask yourself what the most important thing in the world is. If it is your children, then show it. Spend more time with them. Not watching TV but doing things. Teaching and learning from them. Raising children and homeschooling is not anyone's Job. It is Everyone's privilege!

Everyone assumes that Lila does all the home schooling.

I have done a lot of the science, some math, all the shooting and most of the advanced business lessons. She, however, has found a way to take all these crazy and seemingly random lessons that I teach on the spur of the moment and make it fit into a government approved Curriculum. She has taken care of the paperwork every year. I think I only looked at papers required by the state once. That is when I learned they could start getting college credit, paid for by the state, in junior high. Within weeks of learning that, Deven and I met with Kent State University advisors. Deven took tests to get in. Then he signed up for his first college course when he was twelve years old. Apparently, I did not teach him the important parts of what I learned in college. Like what is a reasonable time to start classes. He signed up for an 8 am class. I made it clear that I would do almost anything to help him. I told him he could walk or have mom take him to class that early. Then, I would be happy to pick him up and take him to lunch every day after class. Even after all those years in the Army, I still hate to get up before 8 am.

We all have our strong points and our weaknesses. That is not only OK, it's necessary. If we all were the same, life would be so boring. We need differences. That is what makes us stronger. We should celebrate these things. My wife and I both love our kids. We both really want them to have a good fulfilling life. And I am so grateful that she is so different from me. It makes our marriage exciting. And it allows us to raise our kids and teach them that there are many ways to do the same things.

If you still think that you are not enough, you will grow into that belief. And as soon as you choose to be enough, to be worthy, everyone you need in life will appear. I was raised by a single mom from the time I was about fifteen on. If you are thinking this would be hard for two parents, how can I homeschool my kids all alone and still keep my job? You are correct. It will be harder. But it is worth it! You can do it. And my wife and I found out that no matter how much we knew, no matter how much we cared, it was still not quite enough. We needed the support and love of others who cared for children and education. These people are everywhere. They love to help others, and they really love to help kids. They will be there for you when you need them. They understand that "It takes a village" to train a child.

Whatever you choose to do, traditional school or home-school, I wish you the best of luck. Remember, learning doesn't only happen during a few hours a day. Learning never stops. Actions speak louder than words. If you have people who work for you, you have already trained them. If you have kids, you are already preparing yourself for the lessons you will have to teach to the people you hire. It doesn't matter if you are homeschooling your own kids, if you are a leader in the Army or if you are a business owner. Every day you are called on to teach something. You have to make decisions and take actions. The people around you see these actions and learn lessons. Make sure your actions teach the lessons you want other people to learn. Whether you choose it or not, whether you like it or not, you are already a teacher. Make sure your actions teach lessons that improve you children's lives, your business, and the world.

ERIC'S CHAPTER OUTLINE

- Learning is understanding, not memorizing.
- Learning is more about Why something happens than how it happened.
- You are more qualified than anyone else to teach your own children.
- If all of the evidence points to the contrary, the theory is incorrect.
- Compound interest works both ways...Inflation is negative compound interest.
- Question your assumptions, Especially the ones you know are true.
- The goal of teaching should not be to teach someone everything we know. It should be to teach them to learn. Only then will they learn things that we could never know.
- You can choose easy results, or you can choose extraordinary results.
- Everyone should always be a student and a teacher.
- When you create a new system, don't try to base it on the system you want to replace.

- You can Know everything, or you can Accomplish everything. They are mutually exclusive.

- Some people are happy believing false evidence. Don't try to change them, it won't work.

- Children need their fathers. Step-up and do more than your part of the teaching. Be there for you kids, nothing is more important.

- No one can raise a child or run a business on their own. It takes a village and a team.

CHAPTER 8

Give Them the Strength

ERIC'S EXPERIENCES

When we started in business, I was much more interested than Lila. I had no idea how this was going to end up... I still don't. At the time, I had my business, and she had her job. I saw some other couples struggle with this. It is funny looking back with traditional "Gender roles" It was always the women in my life who had jobs. Not the men. My mom was still working, and my stepdad had retired. My dad hurt his shoulder and had to stop practicing Dentistry when he was much younger than normal retirement age and my stepmom still worked. Then I lost my last job and decided that I was never getting another one. Lila was still working at the animal hospital then. So, it was kind of her job and my business.

I saw the strain this could cause on a relationship where my male friends had real estate, or small (really self-employed) jobs and their wives had "Real" jobs. I wanted to have both a great marriage and a great business. I told Lila that she did not have to help. Just don't hold me back. When I started teaching my kids, I had the same goal. I knew they could learn without me. I also knew Lila and I could teach them many things. Our goal was just to "not hold them back." I did not want them to learn self-limiting beliefs from us. I did not want to teach them how the world was from my point of view. I wanted them to learn how they could make the world better. I wanted to help them grow into the men who would make the world better.

Learning is a natural occurrence. Animals learn what to eat and how to avoid being eaten. Plants learn where the sun is and turn their leaves to face it. We do not need to teach so much. We just need to give our students the tools they need to learn. Unfortunately, the traditional school seems to want to break these tools and throw them away. They can't control people, in school or after they graduate, who have these tools. The school system wants control and obedience. I want creative freedom.

I do not "control" my children or other students. I simply give them the tools to learn. Then I show them that if they use these tools in a positive way that helps everyone, they will be successful at whatever they choose to do. I get them to see why and let them figure out how to do things. This develops their creativity. It gives us both more freedom. It keeps them interested in learning their way, not my way. It is not always the easy way. I frequently see people choose a way that I know is harder. After they fail enough to learn, I give them a nudge in another direction. Notice I did not say the correct direction. I do not assume I know the correct direction. Frequently they move the way I think they should and then totally go off on a wild tangent. The best part is that sometimes the tangents turn out to be way more efficient than anything I knew before.

So not only do I not force control on my kids, I constantly learn from them.

Doing new things is not always easy. It takes courage and strength to get out of your comfort zone. The more stereotypically successful a person is, meaning they have a degree and a 6-figure job, the less likely they are to learn. I did not say that they cannot learn. They are typically great in school. I said that they choose not to try new things. This is not what I see from the ultra-successful. They may have college degrees from an Ivy League School or be a high school drop-out. But they are always trying new ways to do things. They never quit learning.

I want to thank the universe, and my old bosses for firing me three times in two years. I do not differentiate into what words they used. It doesn't matter if I was fired or laid off... One day I had a paycheck and the next day I did not. I now tell people that God pushed me to do more with my life, but I was too dumb to listen. It took three times before I finally got the lesson. I do not know how long it would have taken me to give up a steady paycheck and totally believe in myself. I do know that I decided that my last day at work was going to be a turning point in my life. I decided that I would tell stories about it in years to come and say how it changed my life forever. I was not sure they would have a happy ending. I thought that if all of these things you hear about the law of attraction were true, then I would dive in headfirst. If anyone could "Think & Grow Rich," I could. I decided to make up my own story.

I told everyone around that years from now people would say "Man, he's on fire!" I knew this would become true. I told my friends in private. I sure hope they say, "He took off like a rocket ship" and not "Boy, he went down in a ball of flames." I wasn't sure which of those sayings would describe the next few years of my life, but I knew that I would be on fire. I finally had the incentive I needed to go all in with the next phase of my life. I never questioned if I would have the strength to make it through. There were times over the next five years that I could never have imagined up until then.

That last day at work in 2003 I left and sat at an intersection for a long time. I thought about everything. I especially thought about all of those books I had read, and those tapes and CD's I had listened to driving. If you're too young to remember what those are, it is like a podcast today. I decided I was going all in. Besides, telling your wife that you just started a business is way better than saying you lost another job. I went straight to the bank. I applied for a loan. I told the loan officer that it was the best deal I'd ever found. It was actually. But I had only done one deal before that. I also told him I would know the address by the end of the week. This was before the Great Financial Crisis, so he actually approved me for the loan. Then I went home. When Lila got there, I told her "Good News! I'm a full-time real estate investor."

She said, "Does that mean you lost another job?"

There were nights after that I thought back to what my

dad had taught me as a kid. His lessons weren't always the most fun to learn, but they were useful. He made me tough enough to become an Airborne Sapper in the Army. Trust me, those instructors were nowhere near as scary as my dad. Those were the lessons that kept me going. Between him and survival training, which I ended up teaching, I knew I would never starve no matter what. Lila always liked camping so I knew we would always find a place to sleep. In fact, just a couple years before that we were sleeping on a mattress on a warehouse floor with only a ventless gas heater and a kerosene heater on my side of the mattress. That place got up to about 40 Degrees Fahrenheit at night in December. If we could live through the things we had, we could do anything.

Everyone has had tough times in their life. You can choose to use them as excuses as to why you failed, or you can choose to see how they made you stronger. How they prepared you for the next greater task in your life. And if you are not open to learning these lessons, a higher power may help you learn what you need in unexpected ways. If you believe and have the strength to take action people will appear from places you never imagined to help you succeed. It is amazing how these traits can help you raise kids, start a business and even turn a broken-down warehouse into a home. (Yes, that is where Lila and slept on the floor for about six months in 2000. And then we slept in a bedroom after we had built it for the next five years.)

THE WAREHOUSE

Before

After

I hope my kids never need to survive the way I did. But if they do, I want them to know that they can do it. I teach them in ways that are much more fun. We camped a lot as they grew up. We just went camping last Memorial day. They learned to build fires at a young age. They can use flint and steel and even make a friction fire (rubbing two sticks together.) They are learning what berries they can eat, and how to find the most efficient food sources.

Earlier this year Deven got invited to a conference in Phoenix. The invitation said that since he was underage he was welcome to bring a chaperone. We decided to "rough it" on the way there. We stopped at a small airport in New Mexico for gas. I told him that the airport probably had a car we could borrow. There was a steak house down the road and probably a hotel also. He said no. He would rather camp out. I said that there were comfortable leather chairs and a couch in the FBO. He said sleeping in the plane was fine.

I got out MRE's for both of us. These are not civilian freeze-dried foods. They are military Meals Ready to Eat. They have a shelf life of decades. The first few you eat taste pretty good. Then after you eat the same twelve meals for months at a time you learn to hate them. More than a decade after I left the Army, I still remembered every part and every taste. He got the better one of the two. He even got the best accessory packet. Then after a nice talk I put on a coat and covered up with a light blanket. He didn't bring a heavy coat. I woke up from the cold many times that night. Finally, the sun started coming up. I moved. He moved. Then I asked if he wanted to go in and get a cup of coffee. He couldn't wait.

I was drinking coffee and he was making something hot for himself when he said "You know dad, we could have come in anytime. I was just waiting for you to say you were cold." We definitely have great memories from that night. We got a great story to tell as a bonus. I think he learned a lesson also. And I know he got some of my stubbornness. I should have remembered the night there was a blizzard at one of his Boy Scout "Polar Bear" campouts. It was so bad tents were collapsing. Everyone, including the scoutmaster, moved inside except Deven. He stayed there all night; all weekend. He chose to complete what he started no matter what. His show of strength gave him more strength for the future.

These are some of the ways that we find balance. We have great family moments just traveling to seminars. We tell stories and have fun by campfires. I teach our kids how to live off the land and how to be a businessman. Our whole family built a large greenhouse. Then Lila planted a garden. I dug a pond. Ethan had to save me and the backhoe more than once during that project. Both of them helped and learned to drive the construction equipment. We planted an orchard and vineyards. We keep bees and they all get into bee suits to check out the hives and extract honey. Even their punishments growing up were designed to be positive even if they were negative reinforcement. I had them do push-ups and sit-ups. Sometimes they ran around the drive. Other times they got more work on the farm. All of these things gave them one more tool that they may need to not only survive, but thrive in the future. It helped them to become physically and mentally tough.

I think back to my toughest days. In the worst times I always knew that no matter what, I could hunt and survive off the land. People tell me that they have lost everything. I knew that could never happen to me. I knew no matter what we did, no matter what risk we took, as long as Lila was there with me, I would have everything I needed. When we had Deven and Ethan, I knew that we could always keep them alive and give them the opportunity to thrive. There were times that we could not protect them. But we could feed them and provide shelter. Once you know for sure that you can never lose those things, then you can start working you way up Maslow's hierarchy of needs.

Now I know that my kids are well on their way there. I also know that they have a greenhouse, garden, orchard and a pond. We have enough ammo to feed us for a couple generations. I never expect them to need any of this. I also don't expect them to ever need any of my money, real estate, or businesses. But now that they proved that they really don't need it, when Lila and I are gone, they will be more worthy and qualified to take it and use it to make the world a better place.

ERIC'S CHAPTER OUTLINE

- If one spouse is an employee and the other is a business owner, it can cause stress in the relationship.

- Simply talking and agreeing to not hold each other back will help you grow together, rather than growing apart.

- Learning always happens.

- You can have the illusion of control and obedience, or you can have real creative freedom.
- It takes courage and strength to grow...comfort only holds you back.
- If you conquer the crisis you are living through today it will prepare you for the great success you will have tomorrow.
- Mental and emotional strength is just as important as physical strength.

LILA'S LESSONS

Strength is more than what your muscles can do. I remember Ethan as a young kid trying to lift me up. He was constantly trying to prove that he was as physically strong as his brother at everything they did, even though Deven was older and bigger than he was. What most people need is this strength in their own mind.

Eric had told me of the sign his high school wrestling coach had posted that said, "The mind tires much more quickly than the body." Eric had also told me about one of the first women he worked with in the Army, who literally ran until her body gave out. This was a big lesson for me. I did not realize how weak my mind was at the time. If things got too hard or too uncomfortable, I just wanted to give up. After hearing his stories, I wanted to change this about myself. This had been my introduction to strength of mind.

Growing up, I was a tomboy, and I was very much like Ethan as a kid. If you told me that I can't climb a tree because I was a girl, you would very quickly find me at the top of the tree, just to prove that I could do it. I had my stubborn streak, which depending on when I chose to use it, could be a drawback or a benefit. It made me easy to manipulate, but it also pushed me past some of my fears.

When I was a teenager, I decided that I was afraid of too many things. It started with being afraid to talk in front of groups of people, so I joined acting class to get over my fear of people. When I realized that fear was holding me back from a lot of things and that I could overcome it, I made a list of fears to overcome and began systematically going after all of them.

When I met Eric, one of my fears was heights. He had been a paratrooper in the Army, and, at the time, he was also skydiving in the civilian world. I heard other people make comments about jumping out of perfectly good airplanes, but I knew that I couldn't put down skydivers if I had never actually tried the sport myself. So I made the choice to address my fear by making a skydive.

During my first skydive, I sat in the airplane on the way up and was so afraid, I toyed with the idea of giving up, staying in the plane, and landing in it. Then I saw the girl before me get out, hang on the wing, and give a big smile in to the rest of us before she let go. She really looked like she was having fun! I remember thinking, "If she can do it, so can I!" My stubborn streak took over. So I got out, hung on the wing, gave a big smile in to the jumpmaster, and let go. By the time I landed, I gathered up the parachute, ran into the hanger, and immediately asked "When can I go again?" It was fun! Had I let fear stop me, I would have missed out on a great experience. Now, hundreds of skydives later, I still remember that day and smile! It didn't help me get over my fear of heights, but it did teach me a lot about handling fear and risk.

When Eric talked about us living in the warehouse with no heat in December, he was not exaggerating. Taking on renovating a warehouse was a large project that was definitely outside my comfort zone. But the idea that we could create the house however we wanted was of interest to me. I knew I would learn a lot from the process, and I was truly fascinated by the concept.

I remember my mom and dad coming to look at the building. They walked around as we told them our plans. I knew they weren't sure about this. It wasn't what they would have chosen for me. However, my mom simply looked us both in the eye and said, "Are you sure you can do this?" Eric and I emphatically told her that we could. She immediately accepted our choice and let go of (or at least put aside) her own doubts.

That was my parents. Growing up, I had no curfew. My parents just told me to be responsible. Strangely, just knowing that they were trusting me was enough to make me want to be trustworthy. I asked my mom about this choice after I grew up. She told me that she had given me a good foundation, and by that point, I had to make my own choices. I was amazed by her answer. She truly believed that she had given me the best start she could give and by the time I was a teenager was willing to let me make all my own decisions – including my own mistakes. She had a strength of mind in raising me. I have tried to remember this when I feel the need to be an overprotective parent. Sometimes, we need to put aside our own fears or doubts and let our children make their own decisions so they can learn to make good ones.

I knew our choice of working on the warehouse was a good one. That did not make it easy. There was a steep learning curve for me, and it felt like we worked all day every day. I would go to my job, come home, and work on the warehouse. There were no "days off". We had to get everything done.

In the end, it was my decision to move into the warehouse, even though it wasn't really livable. I had to convince Eric that we should do this. However, we were never in the apartment we had rented except to sleep, and I knew we could sleep in the warehouse. That choice was made in September, so I was not thinking about how cold it would get if we didn't have an operating furnace by December. I thought about how we could use our rent money for extra supplies, how we were spending all our time at the warehouse anyway, and how good it would feel to stay in our own home—one we could eventually own and not one we rented. I knew it would not be comfortable in the beginning, but I thought of it a little like camping.

Most people, when they see where and how we lived, assume that we were just that financially broke and had no choice but to live there. We chose to stay there. Knowing it was our choice did not make it easier to deal with the discomfort or cold, and we didn't have a lot of money back then. We ate Ramen or other inexpensive meals in or, if we did get takeout, got a couple burgers at $1 each. We didn't even have a stove – just a microwave and a Foreman Grill. It was not a fancy life. It would have been considered sub-standard living back then. We didn't even have a working bathroom in the beginning. I had to go up the road to a gas station or visit friends/family to use a bathroom. However, we chose the more difficult road because we knew that, in the end, it was the best choice for us. We thought we would have everything done in just a few months. I didn't realize that it would take over nine months to turn the warehouse into a home. However, looking back, I cherish every memory from that experience.

After we went to the first MMI (Millionaire Mind Intensive) with Peak Potentials, we went back to volunteer with them. I remember sitting in the back, staring at the list of education that they offered, and thinking how amazing our life would be if we could just learn all the lessons Harv had to offer. The MMI had already made an impact in our life, which is why we wanted to come back and help others have a similar impact in their own lives. If we could just take all of Harv's courses, we would be on a rocket ship to success! However, I stared at the page with the list of packages, wondering how we could ever afford to spend $50,000 for the two of us to do this when we were barely scraping by financially. What I didn't know is that, separate from me, Eric had decided that he wanted to do all these classes also. When he came over to me, I mustered the courage to tell him that I wanted to sign up for the Titanium level package, hoping he could help me figure out how to make that happen for us. All he told me was that he had already decided to do that and had talked to the staff about how to split up payments to make it somewhat easier.

Many people look at a situation like that and say, "I can't afford it." That was my first lesson on changing my thought process. It wasn't about "if". The next time you feel like saying "I can't", change your thought process to "How can I?" Had we settled for "I can't" when it came to that education, we would not be where we are now. Some of my best learning came from those courses. It truly changed my world to travel to these events, meet the amazing people that were there, and learn the amazing lessons that truly did change ourselves and therefore our lives. I spent four years in college and didn't get nearly as much value as I got from attending Harv's courses. And I had an amazing and fun time learning the lessons he and the other trainers taught! I remembered wondering why school had never been like those courses!

Now I understand some of the differences. To start,

Harv's courses were very experiential. In other words, you didn't just sit there and learn something. They gave you a little bit of this, but then they would have you out of your seat PRACTICING what you just learned. For a kinesthetic learner like me, that was fantastic! However, the way they ran the events, it didn't matter how you learned best—they addressed every learning method. They encouraged people to work together to achieve better results. In the end, we learned an amazing amount, had a great time doing it, and made some great connections while there. Some of my strength of mind came from some of Harv's events, especially the Enlightened Warrior Camp. Today I still tell myself "Over, Under, Around, or Through—Whatever it Takes, I'll Do!" Harv believed that the reason most people don't succeed is because of the limitations and beliefs in their own mind. He wanted us to improve our "inner game" of mastering our own mind in order to get better results in the "outer game" of the world around us.

When we had kids, I knew I wanted them to be masters of their own mind. I didn't want them to be stopped by fear or limitations of the mind. I wanted my kids to be truly limitless. Some people talk about thinking outside of the box. I wanted my kids to be more like Bill Cook and Pete Fortunato and say, "What Box?" If you don't have a limit in your mind, you will be able to do and create anything.

Our kids have grown up reading books and listening to CD's, podcasts, and speakers who have taught them that anything is possible, that they choose their own results, and that the world needs them to be successful. We have surrounded them with the best people and resources that we could find. These things had a big impact on us as adults, even though we had already formed bad habits and thought processes. Imagine the impact these lessons could have on someone without all our self-limiting preconceived notions. There are enough negative influences in the world. There are people who will tell you that you can't or why something won't work. We wanted to change their narrative to "How can we do this?"

Changing our lives for the better starts with improving our own mind. That is where the real strength is. Even the body builders you see or know have to have a strong mind. It isn't easy to push yourself to be better – whether that is to make yourself physically stronger or to get past a mental barrier. In order to achieve great results, you have to use your mental strength. This is what will keep you moving forward, help you overcome fears and obstacles, and propel you toward success. The key is to never give up, and that takes a lot of mental strength when you are faced with intimidating difficulties. As Harv says, you have to grow yourself to be bigger than the problem. If kids can grow up with the belief that they can overcome any challenge, they will not have to work so hard to grow bigger than the problem. They won't have any limiting beliefs to hold them back.

You know your kids have learned strength when they cannot be corrupted by others. I saw this in Deven for the first time when he was five. We went to a magic show in

Las Vegas, and the magician asked for a volunteer to help. Deven was the first one to stand up and volunteer. The magician asked him how old he was, and Deven told him "Five".

"You have to be six to be on the stage," the magician told him. "Now, tell me again, how old you are."

"I'm five," Deven said honestly. The crowd laughed.

"I'm sorry, then. I'll have to find someone else," the magician told him and then walked away. The crowd, impressed with Deven's courage to stand up and his unwavering honesty, immediately started calling for Deven to be put onstage. The magician allowed him up, and the audience cheered.

The magic trick began with a covered chalkboard hanging above the stage. The magician asked Deven to pick his favorite Las Vegas showgirl from the three on the stage. He picked out the one named Anne Marie. The magician told him that he was going to take Anne Marie out on a date and asked him what they would eat for dinner. Deven told him "hot dogs." The magician then said after dinner they would go back to his place and watch a movie. He asked Deven what movie they would watch. He tried to give Deven multiple ideas of movies he could choose, but Deven thought for himself and answered "Avengers." The magician then said that he and Anne Marie would go to a wedding chapel. He asked Deven if he would marry her. Deven said incredulously, "No. I'm just a kid. I'm too young to get married."

In the end, the chalkboard was uncovered and listed all of Deven's answers, but what I remember most was that the magician was unable to sway Deven into giving a different answer. He was not giving in to peer pressure. He was going to answer honestly and give his own responses. I was very proud of him.

Many people seem to believe that teenagers are more prone to giving in to peer pressure. Now that Deven is fifteen, some people question if he is more likely to follow the crowd. I believe that the stronger someone's mind is as a child, the more likely they are to stay strong when they grow up. Deven had strength of mind, even at the age of five. This summer at Boy Scout camp, some of the kids were picking on him for writing more than one book. To Deven, this is a proud accomplishment, but to those kids, the thought of writing a book was akin to torture. Some teenagers, when faced by negative words from their peers, respond by attacking those peers with other negative words. Deven did not make any negative comments about the kids that picked on him. That's just not who he is. Instead, he showed me that he had emotional strength. It never feels good when someone puts you down for something you are proud of. I thought it was great when Deven made a comment about how their words didn't mean anything to him. He seemed to understand that the opinion of those kids was just that – their opinion. I think, to an extent, he almost felt sorry for them that they didn't understand how amazing his life had become since those books have been published. Since then, he has gotten the opportunity to travel, help and inspire other investors, and speak on the same stage as big names like Robert Kiyosaki, Mark Victor Hansen, George Gammon, and many others! Deven knew those kids would not recognize these names or be impressed with his experiences getting to spend time with them. He had more than just the mental strength to accomplish these things. He had the emotional strength to not let someone else's opinions or words hurt him.

When I was a teenager, had my peers put me down for something that was important to me, I would have felt like less of a person. Deven just felt like they were immature kids who didn't understand and who were missing out on having the same great experiences that he was having. He showed me how mentally and emotionally strong he really is.

Building a team in business, you not only have to have mental and emotional strength to lead, you also want your team members to have these same strengths to accomplish the mission of your business. They need to be open to learning new things. If someone thinks that they already know everything, they will not be a good addition to your business. Markets and information are always changing, and you need team members with the emotional strength to admit that they can always learn something more. Those are the ones that will evolve with the changes and continue to create great results.

Your team members also need to have the mental strength to be able to do what is right when things get tough. If they are lazy or if they give up when faced with a challenge, they will only cause you and your other team members frustration. Find the ones with a strong mind that want to make the parts of the business run well and smoothly. These members also need to have the emotional strength to deal with difficult customers or handle rejection. You need the people who understand that it is not a personal affront when someone says something mean to them. The customer with a complaint is angry or frustrated over the situation even if they make negative personal comments to the team member. You want your staff to be able to diffuse a difficult situation and calm down any unhappy customers. Those with emotional strength will be able to handle these difficult situations with grace.

When our kids originally started buying real estate, I got mixed reactions from the other investors around them. Some people almost ignored them. They might make a comment about it being cute that a kid is attending an event, but then they never actually believed that a kid would use the information that was taught. These were the people that helped Deven, and Ethan gain emotional strength to continue with what they were doing even if these adults did not believe in them or accept them. Other people at these events were amazed. They saw our kids and would talk to them, find out what they were doing, and asked a lot of questions. These people helped Deven and Ethan to gain mental strength, as both kids knew that these other adults would look for them in the future to hear about their progress. It was additional motivation for them to do well and learn more, so they could share their new experiences with these people the next time the kids saw them.

These were the adults that were open to learning new things. One of the reasons Deven enjoys teaching today is because of the adults that talked to him at different events. He loved it when he could teach these grown-ups something that they didn't know. Sometimes he was only teaching what he had just learned so he could understand it better. Other times he was just telling stories about the deals he had done. Either way, these adults were appreciative when he shared a new idea or lesson that he had learned, and this made Deven feel like he was making a difference in the world. Now, he seeks to learn more, do more, and teach more, so he can have an even larger impact on the world.

LILA'S CHAPTER OUTLINE

- Intentionally attack each of your fears and overcome them.

- Overcoming your greatest fears may lead to the most rewarding experiences you ever have.

- If you believe in yourself, you can accomplish anything.

- You have to have the strength to believe in yourself before anyone else will.

- Improve yourself, and you will improve your life.

- You are your biggest obstacle, overcome your own self-limiting beliefs.

- Never give up...have the mental strength to stay true to your word.

- Mental strength is knowing the right thing to do. Emotional strength is doing it even when you peers encourage you to take the easy route.

- Emotional strength allows you to admit your current beliefs are no longer working and change with the markets.

- To be truly successful, you need mental and emotional strength even more than physical strength at times.

CHAPTER 9

Stay Out of Their Way!

ERIC'S EXPERIENCES

In a negotiation, sometimes the hardest thing to do is "shut up." Even if you know that "He who speaks first loses…" You still want to say something. It is just human nature. It is like when you want to show every employee exactly how to do this job your way. Or like when you want to protect your kids. We never mean to hold our kids back. We really want to see them do great things. We may even tell them things like, "When you grow up you can be anything you want. You can even be president." Then in the next breath we tell them, "Stop, you are not big enough." "You need to think realistically." "We can't afford it."

Think of all these terrible, self-limiting beliefs that we put in our kids' heads. We only do it to protect them. We just want them to be safe. Unfortunately, that will keep them right where we are. From the time we had kids, I attempted to teach them to do great things. And even more than that I was determined not to mess them up as much as my parents had. I don't say that to be mean to my parents. There are millions of kids in the world that they only wish they could grow up with parents like mine. Those are just the words that went through my head. "Don't mess this kid up as much as other parents do."

At that time, I had not worked with the great mentors I have now. If so, I would have phrased that in a much more positive way. Even so, it is a true statement. Most of the lessons that we learn from the people who love us the most are taught to keep us safe. They are not taught to help us get ahead. The physiological reason is the medulla oblongata or the reptilian brain. In Maslow's Hierarchy terms, the species cannot go on unless we stay alive long enough to procreate. In emotional terms we love our children and never want anything to happen to them. The real results are that most of the things we teach to keep them safe also hold them back. If we could teach them to do what we have done 10 times as well, we would already be doing 10 times as well. If you teach them to choose between safety and success, they will probably miss both goals.

We end up teaching our children all the things that made us as successful as we are. This is great. We also teach them what things to avoid so they stay alive. Also, a good lesson. Unfortunately, they do not know any better than us which of these lessons really keeps them safe and which ones are just holding them back. If you never do anything new, you can keep yourself very safe. In fact, the safest place on earth is in solitary confinement in a maximum-security prison. I do not want that for me or my kids. Prison is also the place where you have the least freedom. Freedom is really the opposite of safety and security. I choose freedom over safety and security every time. As a soldier I really understand what Benjamin Franklin meant when he said

"Those who would give up essential Liberty, to purchase a little temporary Safety, deserve neither Liberty nor Safety."

If we fight for freedom in all the little ways we do every day, why do we go home and tell our kids to focus on safety? Why don't we tell them to shoot for the stars. Let them know that they will fail over and over. That is OK. Just get up one more time, than you fall down, and you are a success. It doesn't matter how many wrong answers you get if you finally figure out a correct answer. There is no one right answer. There are always many. If we believe that there is only one way to do things, it is only because we have not discovered a better way to do things yet. I had an older contractor doing a job for me. He refused to email me an invoice. He told me "I've been doing this for over thirty years, and I have always hand delivered written invoices." I told him that people rode horses for thousands of years and then they invented the car. If that guy can learn to use a computer, we can all learn to help our children to try new things. We can inspire them to do great things rather than teach to avoid the unknown and strive for safety and security.

Yes, I know, you don't want your kid to fall down. I know the teachers at school say that there is only one answer. I know that you are only as successful as you are because of these things that you learned. Imagine if you had not learned some of these things. Imagine if you had not been afraid or made excuses when you had that opportunity years ago. Imagine how many opportunities you never saw in life because you wanted to play it safe.

Remember what Mark Twain said "It ain't what you don't know that gets you into trouble. It's what you know for sure that just ain't so."

If you want to protect you kids from falling, ask what your success rate is. How many times did they fall before learning to walk? How many scraped knees did you treat when they started riding a bike or skateboard? If you can't protect them from that, why do you think that you can protect them from the rest of the bad things in life? I do not think it is my job to protect my kids from themselves. Sure, I protect them from "bad guys." I teach them to avoid bad places. But most of all I teach them to make good decisions. I let them know their results, good and bad, are their creation. They get total credit for their successes and take full responsibility for their failures. Ask yourself. Is traditional school with one right answer in the back of the book, truly a representation of the way you have experienced the world since you graduated?

Give you kids a chance to fail. If you don't, they will never have a chance to succeed. Quit saying no just because they want to try something new or different. Give them the chance to discover new things. What they find or learn may just make the entire world a better place.

CHALLENGE

I started a challenge. I am determined to make at least 1,000 families financially free in five years. I announced this to the world. I started meetings. I have always done these Wednesday meetings, but now I had a true goal with a timeframe. I wrote twenty-one affirmations. The only price of admission is to read our free newsletter or to show up on Wednesday, read these affirmations out loud and then actually do them every day. (They are listed on my website www.ClearSkyTrainer.com)

Deven was the first person to complete this challenge. Now he is helping me as an instructor and mentor. When he read these affirmations, he noticed something that I had totally missed. Since I have trained him to question every-thing, and he has really learned to see the big picture, he asked a great question. He said "Dad, why do you have to do twenty-one things to become a millionaire but only three things to become a billionaire?"

(Side note: I never teach things that I have not done. I wrote the twenty-one steps to becoming a millionaire. The next three steps came from a billionaire. He would probably say something like "That is the problem with all you millionaires. You keep making stupid millionaire mistakes." He means to play at my level you have to be willing to fail at my level. Or quit holding yourself back… Or some other great piece of wisdom that I haven't quite grasped yet.)

After my fifteen-year-old son found an inconsistency in my teachings I looked closer. Actually, WE looked closer. I knew that the mind that created a problem will usually not be the mind that solves that problem. We found that almost all these twenty-one things have more to do with unlearning than actual learning. They are just to erase the self-limiting beliefs that you have valued for your whole life. Once those are out of the way, there are only a few things you have to do to get everything you want out of life.

I have a list of rules, also listed on my website. I wrote these rules more than a decade ago and still use them today. I teach them to my kids by letting them see the actions I take. When I can't figure out what deal to do or what action to take, I think of this rule.

RULE #1 IS "NEVER MAKE A DECISION BASED ON FEAR."

Ask yourself every time you tell your children something "Am I protecting them and holding them back or am I teaching them to be great?" In the Army we did risk assessments. As a medic I had to know how bad the injuries could be and what was the likelihood of them happening. As a parent I still evaluate things the same way. I let my kids do things when I know that they are going to fall down and get hurt. I do this if I estimate that they will not get hurt too badly. I let them do things that I understand could kill them. (Think about driving a car for the first time.) But this risk is reduced because the likelihood is way lower than them falling off of a jungle gym the first time they try to climb it. For really dangerous opportunities we "Hedge our bets." We wear seat belts and have air bags when we drive. We wear parachutes when doing acrobatics in airplanes. We take water and wear boots when we walk through the desert.

No matter how common or extraordinary an activity is, there is always a way to reduce the risk. Do what you can to protect your kids by reducing the risk. Not by ignoring the risk or trying to eliminate all risk. If you only do what you have always done, you will only get what you have always got. If you want to make your kids just like you, teach them how you did things. If you want them to be great, teach them Why you did things. If you want them to have the tools to become superstars, show them who the people are that are doing things way better than you ever did and then get out of their way! You can't live in fear. If you try to, you will drag you and everyone around you down.

If you know that you cannot trust anyone, no one will work for you for long. If you are the best, you will always have a job, but you will never have a successful business. If there is only one right answer, you will never try to learn more.

I have many good friends and relatives who cannot let go. They have to have control. And they are right. They may be the best in the world at what they do. No one will care as much as them about their business or job. They see this as their greatest strength. I see this as their fear of letting go. I wish that these negative self-limiting beliefs stopped at businesses. It does not. Where do you think they learned that these were good and desirable traits? Almost definitely from the people who loved them the most as they grew up.

I tell students all the time that if they look back, they are almost definitely within 10% of where their parents were at their age. The parents always want them to do a little better. Unfortunately, they succeed. They only make it 10% better in finances, family, and life. What is worse, Generation Z, the kids in America today, are the first generation to believe that they are unlikely to surpass their parents. We have to stop this belief. We have to give these kids hope and not hand-outs. We have to let them fall down and then be there to pick them back up. It is our highest calling to help train the next generation. Not to give them wealth. Not to keep them safe. But to give them the tools they will need when we are gone. It doesn't matter if you are with your son, daughter, nephew, a stranger, or your employees. Everyone that you touch in this world can learn from these lessons.

We need to teach them to see the big picture, not to focus on the little details. We need to show them how to balance work, family, and money. We need to teach them to be motivated and give them encouragement. When they have the strength to make good choices in the worst of times, we can relax knowing that our job is done. With our children and our businesses.

ERIC'S CHAPTER OUTLINE

- Don't teach self-limiting beliefs to your kids or your staff. It doesn't protect them. It holds them back.
- You can have safety, or you can have success.
- Freedom and liberty are the opposite of safety and security. Choose what is more important to you.

- A wrong answer is not a failure, it is just one more way something doesn't work. There is more than one right answer to most problems.

- You can protect them, or you can teach them to take responsibility. Their results, both good and bad, are caused by their choices.

- It is far harder to overcome the self-limiting beliefs we have than it is to learn what we need to grow.

- Never make a decision based on fear.

- You can never avoid all risks, so reduce your risk with education and then have the courage to take the appropriate action despite the risk.

- The world needs hope more than it needs a handout.

- Teach everyone around you to see the big picture.

LILA'S LESSONS

My parents were a pretty good example of knowing how and when to let go and let their children be free, which tested my skills at being responsible for myself and allowed me to fail or succeed on my own terms growing up. I don't remember ever having a bedtime, and, as a teenager, I never had a curfew. Being part of the local acting theater, by the times the shows were over, and we all grabbed a quick bite to eat, I frequently didn't get home until 1:00 in the morning. As long as I kept my grades up, I didn't have a curfew, and, as I previously stated, I was good at playing the memorization game.

When I had kids, I wanted them to have the same experience in this regard. Deven and Ethan choose when they go to bed, and, as long as they are up on time for any scheduled items, this will remain in effect. Neither of them drives yet, but I don't expect to give them a curfew either.

As I learned more about success, I realized that parents can hold their kids back in many ways that are well beyond bedtimes and curfews. I have listened to parents tell their children not to try something out of fear that their kids will fail. For example, one mom at the theater told her daughter not to audition for one of the musicals because she didn't believe her daughter was a good singer. She told her daughter, "Some people just aren't meant to sing." Wow, did that hurt her daughter's feelings. What do you think that young girl learned? I believe it caused multiple problems in that girl's mind, including thinking her mom didn't believe in her, that she wasn't "good enough", and that "why try? I'll just fail." It would have been less damaging to let her daughter audition. The daughter may have gotten the role despite any expectations. Even if she didn't get a role in the play, she would have had the courage to try again later, or it may even have motivated her to learn how to sing better to improve her chances the next time.

Most parents really want to protect their kids from pain. It feels so good to see your child smiling or laughing, and it is akin to torture for a parent to see their child hurting, whether physically or mentally. There are times when the lessons a kid needs to learn are ones that don't feel good to them. For example, it does not feel good when you aren't chosen for a role in a play or aren't picked by a particular sports team. However, telling a kid not to make the attempt can be more damaging than losing to both their self-esteem and their future motivation.

Sometimes, your kids will work to achieve a goal. Maybe they succeed, and maybe they don't. When they don't, be there for them. Help them learn the right lessons, so they are even more prepared to face the next challenge that life throws at them. Remember, our goal as parents is to teach our children to be self-sufficient. When they grow up, they will have challenges and problems in life. They will not always get everything right, and they need to handle those difficult times in a positive way.

Ethan handles a challenge well. He can have someone tell him that something he is striving to accomplish is impossible, but he doesn't stop working to succeed. He doesn't let someone else's limiting beliefs slow him down. He understands that when they say something is impossible, that is just their opinion of the situation. He doesn't accept their opinion as fact. He asks himself how he can make something possible. His dad has always taught him that when someone says, "You can't do that" to think "You're right. You can't do that, but I can!" Sometimes, when I am facing a particularly difficult challenge, I have to remind myself to have the same strong mind that Ethan has. That way I can keep moving forward to find a solution to whatever problem I encountered.

If there are risks involved in an endeavor, we need to teach our kids how to mitigate or lower the risks. When Ethan was 3 and tried to use a blanket for a parachute, with plans to jump off our spiral staircase, I never told him not to skydive. I did explain how the blanket is not a good parachute and that jumping from such a low height would not give a real parachute enough time to open. I explained that he needed to learn the parachute landing fall to help if he has a hard landing. He listened to what I had to say, and we even practiced the parachute landing fall. If you ask him now, he still plans to skydive someday. However, he hasn't tried to jump off the stairs again with a blanket. I wanted him to learn to think through a way to do something that reduced the risk of him getting hurt. I did not want to limit his thinking or teach him that he should not take on a challenge.

If your child wants to climb a tree, what do you tell them? Do you tell them not to do it because you are afraid they will fall? Do you tell them to do it but not go very high? Or do you explain how to pick a tree that has branches strong enough to hold them, explain how to find good handholds and places to put their feet, teach them about having 3 points of contact, and encourage them to climb higher?

I was constantly climbing trees as a kid. I loved figuring out how to get up in them, see how high I could make it, and then enjoy the view. Did I fall out of any trees? Yes. I did not break any bones, but I did have some decent bruises and scrapes. It never stopped me from climbing another tree. I even figured out how to shimmy up some that didn't have low branches to use. Did I worry my parents? Probably. I remember my dad yelling at me for climbing a tree in a dress, to which I promptly responded, "Then don't put me in a dress!" (They'd made me put one on for some event we were going to.) I remember my dad talking about falling off our roof and breaking his wrist. I think he was trying to tell me to be careful when climbing the trees. To his credit, he never told me not to do it. I do not, however, remember him encouraging it either. Sometimes, I wonder what it may have changed for me if he had. Would I have ended up as fearless as Ethan?

We need to help our children have courage in taking on challenges in life. They need the self-confidence to know that, even if some tasks seem difficult, they can figure out a way to make it work. There have been many "impossible" tasks that a strong mind proved was possible. One example used frequently is running a mile in under 4 minutes. People said that was impossible until Roger Bannister accomplished this in 1954. Another example is separating conjoined twins and having both twins survive the surgery. At one point in our history, parents had to make a heartbreaking decision on which twin they would save. Then, in 1987, Dr. Ben Carsen figured out a way to do the surgery in which both twins survived. Since then, he has helped several other families with this same situation. We can use real life examples like these to demonstrate to our children that nothing is impossible. We just have to figure out how to make something possible.

When Ethan first started washing his own laundry, he was not very tall. He had to open the dryer, lift himself up until his feet were off the ground, open the washer, and then essentially lean into it with his feet in the air to get his clothes out of the washer. Then he would rock back slightly, put the clothes in his other hand, and then throw them into the dryer. Then he'd rock forward again and grab more wet clothes. He'd repeat this until everything was transferred to the dryer. He never complained or thought to admit that he was too short to do the job. He maybe should have thought about moving over a chair or step-stool. However, he figured out a way to get his clothes washed and dried that worked for him.

As parents, we need to let them figure things out for themselves. We can coach, guide, and assist when they ask for help. We need to encourage them to think through their own problem-solving. Let them know that you believe in them and their ability to accomplish great things. They may surprise you with how adept, creative, and inspiring they can truly be!

LILA'S CHAPTER OUTLINE

- Responsibility can only be learned if you have freedom to choose.
- Most of our self-limiting beliefs are based on the fears of our loved ones.

- Not trying because you might fail is more damaging than trying and failing.

- Don't protect your team or your family from every possible failure, just be there to help them up if they get knocked down.

- Learn to mitigate risk so you can grow bigger than the risk.

- Many tasks that once seemed impossible have already been overcome by strong minds.

- Give people the freedom to be as creative as possible and their solutions may inspire you.

CHAPTER 10

Congruence in the Big Picture... Synergy

ERIC'S EXPERIENCES

When I was training to be a speaker for Peak Potentials there was a huge focus on being congruent. I knew what that word meant in geometry. It did not seem that difficult. The more I learned, the more I applied it to my own life. The more I applied it to my own life, the more inconsistencies I found. This may have been one of the most important lessons that I had to learn to get out of my own way. It is also one of the things that I have worked on the most. You cannot teach this or tell it. You have to live it. When the people around you see you being dishonest with yourself in any way it causes tension and doubt. When every one of your thoughts, feelings and actions are pointing in the same direction, others see this and believe in you. What is more important, you believe in yourself more completely than you ever have before.

It is not that easy to define congruence in simple terms. It is to get every action to move you to the same goal. It is getting every thought to move you toward those actions. It starts with your feelings and beliefs. It is the exact words that you use. It is the jokes that you tell. It is how you present yourself. More than that it is the sum of these things matching each other.

Dr. R. Buckminster Fuller, the futurist, inventor and the "Planet's Friendly Genius" was a teacher and mentor to many of my mentors. He called this synergy. Synergy is the behavior of whole systems. Many people say that the whole is greater than the sum of the parts. The traditional school system still tries to teach each of the parts and then students don't understand why they cannot see the big picture. Students ask, "When am I ever going to use this in my life?" They are forced to memorize parts with no understanding of the whole. If you want your children, students, or staff to have more motivation show them the big picture. Let them be creative. Let them use their imagination. When they see the big picture, they can become more congruent and less fragmented. They will start to see how their part fits in with the rest of the team's contributions. Then your whole family or team will have more synergy.

All parts of your team must work together for the same goal. And all parts of you must work toward the same goal. First you must recognize that you cannot get to any goal unless you clearly define what that goal is. Everyone should have hundreds of goals written. You should have time frames. A goal without a deadline is just a dream. Once you have that goal you must make sure it is clear, precise, and measurable.

You cannot achieve a goal of being happy. Happy is a state of mind. You can choose to be happy or not. You also cannot get "Rich." But you can become a millionaire. Or a billionaire. My favorite dream is when people tell me "I just want to be comfortable." That is impossible to measure. How will you ever know if you are there. Is the goal a better pillow or a new chair? What if you change your mind. We live in the United States. Other nations are shocked by us because our poor people have enough food to get fat. To many millions of people on earth, just living here makes you way more "comfortable" that anyone they know. So, when you set your goals choose something measurable. Pick something that is achievable—something that will drive you. And when you grow yourself to be more congruent, you will attract others that are also congruent. That is the synergetic team that can accomplish anything. And, when your kids see this, they will start thinking, talking and acting congruently.

It is interesting how people always tell you exactly what they are going to do. In five minutes, I can tell you if a person is Poor, Middle Class or Rich. You can give the first one of these people a million dollars and take everything from the last one and in a few years, they will be right back in the same place they started. When I was working with the British Paratroopers, they found it amazing, or possibly just weird, that we could change social classes. One even said, "You Americans, not only do you allow someone to move up in class, you actually celebrate it when they do." At the time I was shocked that so many people in the world really thought like that. Now I see that, at least in the United States, it is more the individual person holding themselves back, than it is someone else pushing them down. I have meetings all the time where multiple great deals are offered. Some of these deals are no money down. When the people who never buy them leave they say, "I don't know why no one will give me a chance." I have always taught my kids that opportunity doesn't knock. It sneaks past the door. All you have to do is be there when it does and take action. In fact, when they were in the Knock-Knock phase of joke telling, we had a favorite joke.

Knock-Knock. Who's there? Opportunity. Opportunity Who? WHY would you question opportunity!

This later got shortened to: Knock-Knock. Who's there? Opportunity. Well come on in!

What was a kid's joke became real life for some people. Some of the highly educated and specialized people that we meet can sit at the same table as my teenagers and never see an opportunity. Then they are shocked the next week when one of my kids tells them about this great 4-unit they just got under contract or closed on. When the adult asks where they found that great deal, they respond, right here last Wednesday night.

My children are not any smarter that the others. They are just more open-minded. They always see opportunities until they prove that it is not a good deal. Others are so conditioned from living the life they expect to happen to them that they only see problems. They know that nothing is a good deal until they exhaust every possible way it could go wrong. By then someone else already took the opportunity.

Being congruent means saying you are an investor and then investing in things. If you show up late to a meeting with me and then ask to borrow money, I am going to see a person who is late. If you do not care about my time or your commitments, you will probably not pay me on time. If you can't figure out why no one believes that you are a professional, look down at the T-shirt, holey jeans and flip-flops you are wearing. If you want to be a professional look and act like one. If you want lenders to believe that you will pay on-time, show up on-time. If your word means nothing to you, why should it mean anything to me?

If you go way out of your way, at great personal cost, to accomplish some small task just because you agreed to do that task, I will see that. Like Harv always said, "How you do anything is how you do everything."

This works in both positive and negative ways. The more you think positive thoughts and take positive actions, the more positive things will happen to you. Some people say, "The more I prepare, the luckier I get."

The more you blame, justify, and complain, the more problems you will have. I just ordered more business cards. Yesterday they came in for the third time. This time they were not only the wrong color, they were also off center. I took them back and the guy behind the counter was complaining that he had been there for years and kept getting passed over for promotion. He wanted his boss's job, and he deserved it because of his time there. I handed him the third set of cards that had been printed with purple ink rather than blue. He immediately had a string of excuses. Then he very persuasively placed the blame on his supplier. I wanted to explain that if I were his boss, I probably would not promote him unless he started taking responsibility. I also realized that he was happier where he was than if he got the promotion and had to take the responsibility. No matter what his circumstances, I was sure he was not open to my opinion. So, I told him to let his boss reorder the cards and send them to my office.

There are so many ways that people sabotage themselves. Most of them are because they are not congruent. I have always taught my kids that everything was their fault. I told them that if it was someone else's fault, they had no control over the outcome. But, if they could find some way that they could take responsibility, then they could have control. I also made sure they knew that every good thing that happened in their life was also their creation. You cannot have the yin without the yang. You cannot take credit for your successes and blame your failures on someone else. If you try, your subconscious will stop you. This may cause self-doubt. It may present in many ways. The one thing it will not do is help you learn and grow. If you are in control of your life, then you must take responsibility for your actions and results. Not just the ones that work out for you.

Some of the most common incongruencies I see are wasting time on things that really are not important. It is not necessarily what you are doing that is a problem. It is what you are not doing. You may just hang out for an hour or two at the bar or golf course or wherever you like to go with your friends. Some of these things are healthy and good ways to not only relax but to network and grow. And when you go home and complain about not having any money even though you just spent $50 on beer you may see some inconsistencies. If you watch TV for hours every night and then turn down a Saturday shift or a new client to spend time with your kids, there may be an inconsistency. There is abundance in life. There is always enough time. You just have to allocate it wisely. You could take the Saturday shift, go out with your friends one evening and still play with your kids every night without the TV on. There is always enough of what you want and need. You just have to get rid of some of the less important stuff in your life.

In my last post in the Army, I was an instructor. I was in the Reserve then and had to travel a couple hours to my duty station on the weekends where I worked. Many of us went out every Saturday night since we were in a hotel away from our families. At the last one of these dinners, we had the same conversation as always. One of the other instructors would say they didn't have any money. Another would start complaining about the same thing. Eventually I would ask about their hobbies. Then I would tell them how they could turn that into a business and make more money doing what they loved to do. One of these instructors loved to bake. She made impressive wedding cakes. I could not believe how much she sold them for. She wanted a second oven in her kitchen but said she could not afford it. The solution seemed easy to me. The cost to buy and install another oven would be paid for in five or six cakes. From then on it was almost all profit. Her response was "Wohlwend, can't we make it through a single meal without you talking about business?" A perfect example of incongruence is when you keep complaining about a problem and then choose to ignore a solution to that problem.

There is abundance in life. There are plenty of opportunities. You just have to be the right person in the right place at the right time. Being the right person means that you are open to solutions. It is very hard to do that if you do not have a well-defined goal. Why would you try new things if you don't even know if they will get you something you want?

A great way to confuse people is to change the definition of words. This is happening more and more lately. Liberal is from the Latin "Libre" which means Free; but the "Liberal" political party seems to want to take away more of my freedoms than the other party. When I studied medicine, we had a definition for a vaccine. Now it is totally different. Just last week they changed the commonly accepted definition of a recession. Do they think, if we get rid of words in our language that we don't like, nothing bad can happen? Do they think that we will really start believing these things even though our other senses tell us the opposite? I do know this sounds a lot like the "Newspeak"

that Orwell wrote about. I also know that far too many people believe these new definitions.

If we can change the definition of a word, it is very hard to be congruent. You can confuse everyone around, including your own mind, if you do not use words the way you understand them. If your mind still thinks in the "outdated" definition of words, your actions may be completely inappropriate.

For instance, if you know what a man is, if you know there have been males and females for thousands of years, and then you hear a supreme court justice say she does not know what the definition of a woman is, it may be confusing. Does she really not understand this basic concept? That seems completely unlikely. She is smart enough to achieve this high position so she must be pretty smart. Is she blatantly lying? She is in the highest job in the country. The supreme court's mission is to find the truth. If you choose a judge that lies out of convenience it would be bad. Does she intentionally use incongruent words to push her own personal ideas on the rest of society? I am sure there are many innocent explanations. There are many terrible theories also. It is not her beliefs that are good or bad for the nation. It is the confusion her words create in our own minds that is driving people apart.

Imagine if you did that in your own home. If you tell your kids not to jump on the bed one day and then the next day, they see you jumping on the bed, what will they learn? They will learn that your words and actions are not congruent. What if you just told them not to do something one day, and the next day you chose to do what you told them not to do. Many parents or bosses have different rules for themselves than for their kids and staff. I have heard parents say things like "You can do anything in life... but never do what I do for a living." Then the next day the parent got up and went to work to do that same job again. Now the kids see that your words are not congruent. Do you see how this may be confusing? This sends mixed messages and makes it hard to learn what lesson you are trying to teach. It would be like hearing a reporter talk about peaceful protests while you watch a cop car burning in the background. It is hard enough to be congruent in this world. Using words in a way that we know is incorrect makes being congruent almost impossible.

If you really want to confuse someone, just change the definition of a word. One day not too long ago the definition of Inflation was "Swelling; increase in the amount of fiduciary (paper or token) money issued, beyond what is justified by the country's tangential resources; a rise in prices." Then they changed the dictionary. They left out the whole middle part about increasing the monetary supply. Now they want us to believe that the effect is the cause. If you cannot differentiate the cause from the effect, you cannot be congruent. If the definition of words can change to mean the opposite of what it was before, or if a word started meaning the cause and now is defined as the effect, how much confusion will it cause in the world?

These are the things that we teach our children. We teach them the old words and the new. We teach them to dissect the root of words and ask why they do not match the current definition. I, and my children always ask, "If this action happens, who gains something?" Just like in business, if you follow the changing rules, you will see where people are leading you. If you follow the money, you can generally see why something is happening. And if you follow the outdated definitions of words, you will probably see where someone is trying to take advantage of you.

Let your kids and your staff know exactly where they stand. Don't hide it from your tenants when you are selling a building. People make better decisions than the world gives them credit for. But they can only make a decision if they have actual facts. If they are confused, they almost always say no, hide or avoid the situation. I see many investors ask for owner financing and the sellers say no. The main reason they say no is because they do not understand all of the benefits to them. The investor may use technical words that confuse the sellers. This does not make you sound smart. It makes your counter party feel inferior and more likely to just avoid the whole situation. In business and parenting there are many good answers to problems. Some are better than others, but many different solutions can work. Do your best to explain the circumstances to your counter party. Help them understand why you want to do something. Use clear and concise words. Your kids are more likely to learn the lesson you want them to learn.

Sellers are more likely to accept your offer, and your staff is more likely to get what you want done on time, on budget and at the right quality.

On the opposite side of the coin, people are being taught in school that there can only be one answer to a problem. There may be many answers to a problem. But we can never find or agree on them if we use different measuring sticks, or if we change the meanings of words. Albert Einstein said, "Problems cannot be solved with the same mindset that created them." We need to be creative. We need to think differently. We need to embrace others' ideas as well as our own. This diversity should draw us together and make us stronger. It should not divide us. If you are speaking and acting on your beliefs, and you are congruent, others' beliefs will not bother you.

Ayn Rand said "There are no contradictions. If you find a contradiction, then you should check your premises. One of them is incorrect."

To be totally congruent you must see the big picture. You must look at yourself from other people's point of view. Most people do not do this. Some people do not understand why they can't get others to see their point of view. It may be because they are trying to force their point on someone else. If you want to be good at negotiating in a business deal, or with a 2-year-old, you need to see what they want first. I remember when a city council was trying to pass an ordinance that would be bad for landlords. I watched other landlords stand up and say they were too poor to afford this new registration fee. I watched how a couple of the city council members reacted. I do not care how broke you are. When a council person who has rented their whole life sees that you not only own a house, but you also rent your second house to others, it is not in their belief system to see that you are broke. It does not matter if you need a new $10,000 roof and your tenants are not paying. It does not matter if you are way over-leveraged. What some other people will always see is the rich landlord who will not pull their fair share.

It doesn't matter if this is correct. It really does not matter if it is right or fair. It is just a fact. You cannot change people's opinions until you show them a new way of thinking. I could not change the school system as a teacher. I could not change it by volunteering to donate time and better books and materials. So, I decided to build a better system that people can choose to use. This will make the old system and ways of thinking obsolete.

I have grown to be much more congruent than I was before. I will always keep learning and growing in this direction. I have defined, explained, and then shown my kids how to be congruent by the choices I made and actions I took in my Life. I have done my best to teach my kids what congruence is. Only they can learn to be congruent in their own lives. It is not something that can be taught to you. But it is something you can learn. Once you do become more congruent in your life, you will find more people like you. They will make it even easier to move up to the next level in every area of your life.

You have to see the whole picture to become totally congruent. I don't know if any of us will ever have that ability, but the closer you get the more the universe lines up to help you. The more synergy you and your family and team will have. That will allow you to achieve bigger and better goals.

ERIC'S CHAPTER OUTLINE

- The whole is only greater than the sum of the parts if all the parts add to the whole.
- You cannot see the big picture by memorizing a picture of each of its parts.
- You cannot reach a goal until you clearly define the goal.
- Goals must be measurable and have a timeframe.
- When all your traits align toward the same goals, when you become more congruent, you will draw others to you that are working for the same goals you are.
- When like-minded, congruent people work together, the synergy of the team can overcome almost any obstacle.
- If you expect to see opportunities, you will. If you expect to have problems...You will get those too.
- Your results come from your actions and appearance, not just your words.
- Take responsibility for every part of your life.

- Every time that you blame, justify, or complain, you are giving control of your life to someone else.

- Everything is abundant if you allocate it correctly.

- You cannot make informed decisions if the definitions of words are changed.

- Some systems cannot be fixed. You must build a system so much better that it replaces the old one.

LILA'S LESSONS

I am one of those people who is content to sit and do very arduous, detailed work. For example, my dad used to create these 2-inch-tall animals out of wood, and I would paint them, complete with eyes and other tiny features. They were cool to look at, but the time investment was not worth what he could sell them for. However, he liked to make them, and I liked to paint them. While this was great for spending time with my dad, this was not a useful skill when it came to running a business.

In business, being able to focus on very small details was much less useful to me. Eric told me for years that I needed to see "The Big Picture." At the time, I didn't really understand what he meant. I thought I did at times, believing that knowing there were multiple different departments or parts in my business was enough. Then I would wonder why things weren't working out or why I couldn't seem to plan ahead. I felt like I was constantly reacting to situations instead of being able to prevent problems. When

I would talk to Eric about my frustrations, he would tell me to look at the Big Picture.

I originally pictured it to be like a jigsaw puzzle. You could see from the top of the box what it should look like when you are done, and you knew the pieces to that picture were inside. I sort of understood that how you organize those pieces is what helps you to get it to look like that outside picture. However, I was missing something. Eric tried to explain multiple times, but I didn't understand why the picture in my head didn't work. What was this "Big Picture" if it wasn't the completed jigsaw puzzle that I thought it was?

At some point, I was so frustrated at hearing the same thing, I stopped trying to figure out what Eric meant. I worked on trying to improve the processes for finding new customers or for handling emergencies. I would focus on one department and get it going. Then I'd move to the next one that was having problems. However, by the time I'd thought I had the second department going, something else was broken. None of my efforts seemed to help.

I blamed it on my skills at hiring or training. I worked to get "better people" on the team. All the time, Eric kept telling me to look at the Big Picture. After a while, I began to hate that phrase, and I couldn't figure out why my brain couldn't grasp the concept.

What was worse, my kids started to understand him. For example, when Deven bought his first house, he had plenty of equity but no cash flow. After discussing this with his dad, who told him that he needed to look at the big picture, he immediately decided to buy a mobile home. That got him the needed cashflow to keep his company running smoothly. I thought the lesson was to focus on or buy what you are missing. That's what I was doing! Why wasn't it working? I should have seen how the one deal compliments the other.

Then one day, Eric used a new word. He started by telling me to see the Big Picture, and I reminded him that I don't understand what he means when he says that. Then, he told me to read about Synergy. I said, "That's how things work together. What does that have to do with the Big Picture?" No sooner were the words out of my mouth, I understood completely.

I had gotten my jigsaw puzzle, knew what the box looked like, and kept trying to organize the pieces. However, I wasn't figuring out how they all fit together. I was just matching similar colors where I thought they should go. Then, those loose pieces, even if they may be in nearly the right position, never stayed in place because they weren't connected to anything else!

I realized that the Big Picture isn't just about looking at all the parts and knowing that they belong together. It isn't just about seeing what you want it to look like in the end. It is about how all the pieces fit together and work together. I had been missing the connection between all of the parts. Seeing the big picture is about understanding how everything works together.

I had been so stuck on my preconceived notion of what I thought the Big Picture should be, my mind turned off any other possibilities, no matter how many times Eric tried to explain it to me. My kids got it, however. They didn't have any prior idea to be stuck on. This is why it is easier to teach kids than adults. Adults have to spend a lot of time unlearning the things they thought to be true in order to learn new things. They need to learn to let go of prior beliefs and question every single premise they have.

It wasn't until Eric accidentally chose the right word that he forced my brain to think beyond my preconceived notions. My mind asked "Why hadn't he used that word before? That could have saved me a lot of time, headache, and hassle!" However, the problem was all in my own brain. Eric had explained it over and over, and I would try to make his words fit what I wanted them to mean, even if that wasn't even close to what he was trying to tell me. I needed to let go and look at it differently.

Now that I get the concept, I can look back at many things I did wrong in my business. One of the big ones of which was doing too much of the day-to-day work. No one can see the big picture if they are focused on the minute details. In my business, I was so busy "painting" small details daily, just like I did on those little wooden animals. Meanwhile, major problems were occurring around me that I was too busy to notice. Then, I would wonder why my team wasn't getting the right results!

Another problem was that I wasn't good at letting go

and trusting my team members. I would do something because I thought it was faster for me to do it than to try to teach someone else to do it. However, then the team was depending on me for these items. If I was not available when they needed one of those items done, the task would sit there waiting for me, no matter how important it was to accomplish now. I was my own bottleneck. I needed to let my team members learn and empower them to take action.

One of my biggest issues was that I wasn't enforcing the use of our great systems manual. My team members learned that it was easier to ask me how to do something than to look it up. I finally hung a sign on my office door and then closed it. The sign said, "If you have a question, first get the systems manual and turn to the page that has the answer to your question on it. Then you can ask me." It's funny how they had so few questions when that sign was up. The next week, even with the sign down and my door open, I still saw them with the manual, and they had very few questions.

The biggest lesson I learned was in relation to a board in our office. Eric had encouraged me for years to keep track of the team's statistics. I did this, but it was on a spreadsheet in my computer. I tracked things, but I did not look at them frequently nor know how to use all that information to my advantage. Then, after I was gone for a week volunteering at Boy Scout summer camp, I returned to the stats written on a white board in our conference room. Eric walked me through how he saw that board. Once I understood what it all meant, I wondered how we ever lived without that board. Now, we have a system for exactly what to do if a single number drops below its expected value. That one board tells me where problems are in the business and what we need to change to get it back on track. We update some of the numbers daily and the other few weekly, so we have the opportunity to react quickly to problems. The faster we can catch an issue and adjust, the smoother things go.

Life is full of great lessons like these. Every lesson you learn in life advances you forward, but life is not a flat landscape. These stages are more like stairs, so every advancement is like jumping up a step. Then you may walk forward and hit the riser of the next step. It may take a while (and sometimes more than one lesson) for you to make it up to the next step. In order to get there, you will have to see a bigger picture and grow your mind to make it there. There will always be another step to climb. This is why it is important to work with a mentor who already is where you want to go. They know what it takes to get to the stair that they are standing on. If you move fast enough and make it to standing on the same step as that mentor, it is time to find another mentor that can help you climb up higher.

One of the men Eric is mentoring was surprised to find out that we still use mentors at our stage. However, we need these leaders that think bigger than us and are many steps beyond where we are to teach us and inspire us to keep climbing. We have many great people who are currently working with us and inspiring us to move forward and accomplish great things! If you want your own path to be easier, find a mentor to help you. Don't wait for some event to do this. Start now. Too many people are stuck waiting for something, and it only holds them back.

Remember that life is a journey, and you need to keep moving. Many people seem to be looking for some ending point where they can stop learning, working, or striving for something better. Some people think if they make "enough money", they will reach a point where they will never have to do anything again. Others talk about retirement as if that is an end point. They'll say things like "When I retire, I'm going to travel and see the world." They'll make plans with their spouse, and both will wait for this "end point." My mom and dad did this. They knew it was only a few more years to retirement, and then they had plans for travel and time together. Then, my dad was diagnosed with Cancer and was gone in nine months, just three years before he was going to retire. They waited and never got to enjoy those goals. Eric's dad and his wife did the same thing. They waited until she retired to travel in their motorhome, only to have the heartbreak of having to return early due to his health issues.

Why do we wait to do things we want to do? I can't help but think of Dr. Seuss's book *Oh The Places You'll Go*, where he talks about the waiting place:

...For people just waiting.
Waiting for a train to go

Or a bus to come, or a plane to go
Or the mail to come, or the rain to go
Or the phone to ring, or the snow to snow
Or waiting around for a Yes or No...
Everyone is just waiting...

Why are people waiting? Why do they think that we should, at any point, stop growing ourselves? I can't imagine not wanting to learn more, do more, and see more. To me, the day I stop learning or striving to do more and be better is the day that I die. I believe what most people really want is Freedom to do more of what they want in their life. It doesn't matter if that is to travel, build a house, or start a new hobby. You don't have to wait for retirement or some "end point" to do these things. The question is, how can you accomplish these goals and integrate them into your life now? If you need more money to do these things, figure out how to make the money. If you need the time, determine how you can make the time to do them, like hiring more people and delegating tasks to them.

I love my memories of my adventures with my husband. Whether we were skydiving, scuba diving, white water rafting, seeing the Grand Canyon, or simply reading and discussing books by the pool at a hotel, every moment and memory is precious. We haven't waited to do the things we wanted to do. Sometimes, we did have to plan a way to get what we wanted. That has only helped us grow in our knowledge of how to accomplish something. It has given us a Why to drive us forward.

What goal are you waiting to achieve? Who can help you get there? You can start this right now. As Deven would say, "The best time to plant a tree was twenty years ago. The next best time is today, so, be creative and take action!"

LILA'S CHAPTER OUTLINE

- The "Big Picture" is more about how the pieces fit together than it is what it looks like at the end.

- If you can't hire good people, you may want to look at your leadership.

- It is not what you are missing; it is getting the people or parts that you already have to complement each other.

- The big picture is Synergy.

- If you already know, if you have a preconceived notion, you cannot learn any more.

- If you don't empower your team, you will be your biggest bottleneck.

- The better you track every part of a business, the easier it is to see the big picture of the business.

- Growth happens in a punctuated equilibrium. It is like a staircase. You can run across one step until you hit the next riser. Then you need to grow before you can start running again.

- The best time for anything is now...do not wait!

CHAPTER 11

Stay Focused & Tell Positive Stories

ERIC'S EXPERIENCES

When I was working with Peak Potentials, Robert Riopel was one of their trainers. Rob had been with the company for a long time. He really lived the lessons that we were teaching. When you are on stage in front of that many people, some of them put you on a pedestal. Rob never acted like there was any difference talking to one person than one thousand. Every single student was as important to him as a huge crowd or a multi-million-dollar business partner. I remember taking a good friend from home with me to an MMI event. Rob asked if we wanted to get dinner that night. I told Aaron and his wife to meet us at dinner. We were eating with Rob. Aaron and his wife, showed up a few minutes late. He said he had to get a shower after that long day. As soon as Rob walked away to get something Aaron said, I can't believe that it is just the three of us couples. I thought you meant there would be fifty of us here.

Rob came back with our drinks or whatever it was that he thought could make our lives better. He sat there and was so focused on us that the whole restaurant seemed to disappear. That is what he always does. There can be thousands of people in the room. There a can be a dozen things breaking and going wrong. And if he is talking to one student or one couple, he never loses focus. He absorbs what is going on, but the whole time those people feel like they are the only ones in the universe when they talk to him. Aaron still remembers this years later. How Rob made him feel at that dinner that night.

****

ROBERT RAYMOND RIOPEL

Over the past 20+ years I have been blessed to not only share the stage with some of the top thought leaders on this planet, I have also been able to sit down with them in the green room or over dinner to find out who they truly are at their core. I also look for CLUES to their success so that I can model in my own life as well as teach others what I learn.

As I have been studying this amazing book I have been doing the same thing, looking for the CLUES to their success and I have not been disappointed, so the first thing I would like to say is

Thank you Eric, Lila, Deven and Ethan for who you are and the examples you are leaving all around you.

This leads me to one of the biggest CLUES I have noticed in their journey as a family.

Who are you surrounding yourself with???

There is a powerful statement that I have believed in and followed for years that says "Surround yourself with like-minded people". In fact, from the stage I often ask my audiences how blessed they feel being in a room full of like minded people? They are always excited at this fact just as I was.

It was not until one of my mentors (have you studied chapter 6 of this book?) taught me a lesson that was a paradigm shift for me just 2 years ago.

Here is what he said

Robert, if you are surrounded by like-minded people and those people happen to be complainers, what do you think you will be doing? The answer in that moment was obvious and knowing that there was a deeper lesson here because he would not just leave me struggling with that realization, I asked.

Who should I be surrounding myself with?

His suggestion was that I surround myself with "Growth-Minded" people. I was not sure what the difference was, and he could see the confused look on my face so he explained. A growth-minded person will be there to celebrate your successes with you as well as to help lift you up when you stumble or fall, however, the most important role that they will have is to be **willing** (notice this word) to have those tough conversations with you when needed. Things like;

- Why are you playing small right now?
- What was your biggest lesson from that disaster and more importantly what will you do differently because of the lesson?

- Why are you being a jerk right now?

I will never say that it is easy having these kinds of people in your life, but I will tell you it is worth it. Just look at the multitude of lessons that Deven and Ethan have learned because of who Eric and Lila are and the way they live their lives by example.

I will end my narrative by saying this. I would not be writing these words for you to read right now. I would not be doing what I love impacting people around the world, if it was not for one of these Growth-Minded people that I am blessed to have in my life. That person is my amazing wife, Roxanne.

You see, left to my own devices I would not be where I am today. Instead, I would be comfortably miserable in a job. Growing up I was raised to find a stable job that will support your family, even if you do not like it. Why? Because that is what you do. Roxanne however has never been willing to let me play smaller than I am, even if it means giving me a swift kick in the butt sometimes because I am resisting and trying to play small.

As the saying goes "Your playing small does not serve the world".

Eric, Lila, Deven and Ethan, keep being the examples that you are. Letting the world see that you are human like everyone else, that you have faults, that there are things that you do not know and that you are willing to not let this hold you back. Keep surrounding yourself with those

Growth-Minded individuals that will continue holding all of you to the higher standards just like you do each other. You are all blessings to this world and it is a better place because you are here.

— Robert Raymond Riopel, bestselling author and podcast host of *"Success Left A Clue"*

****

After working with so many incredible people I have seen that most of them are like this. Sure there may be 10% that are high maintenance. But most really want to make the world a better place. They truly care about you. Stewart Welch wanted to be a trainer for Peak Potentials. I got to know him when he first started there. He was in a league way above most of the rest of us starting out. He had already published half a dozen books. He was on Fox News for a financial update every week. He owned and ran a huge hedge fund. And he really did not enjoy sleeping in the woods on the ground.

Every time we talked, we would have a great conversation. Then I would say something limiting and Stewart would hold his hands apart as far as he could and tell me to "Think Bigger." When we were in the mountains of British Columbia, I told Stewart, I know why I am here. *(I wanted to learn what these great people did and how they did it. I also really enjoyed the crazy things that Harv had us doing.)* So I told Stewart, "You don't enjoy this camping stuff. You already make a million a year. Why would you want to be out here doing all this crazy stuff?" I'll never forget his answer.

He said, "Because I want to make a million a month and this is where I will meet the people who will take me there."

I knew that the Why was way more important than the How. This is when I started to learn that the Who was much more than the how or the why. The Who, or the people that you spend your time with shape you into who you become. The who that you are helping give you direction. The Who in your family give you drive. It is always about the people. Never about the widget. People always say "If I could just come up with 1-million-dollar idea…" It is never the idea. It is more than 90% the people who can implement that idea that makes it valuable. There are million-dollar ideas everywhere. Finding people who can take an idea and turn it into a product or service successfully are what create that million dollars.

You need these people on your team. No, don't put off your business until you can find a famous person to be your friend. Get started now! Once you create a product or service that can change the world, you will find them. The saying goes "When the student is ready, the teacher will appear." That is true. But they do not normally appear in your living room. While some of these people have come to my house, and I have gone to many of their homes, I originally met all of them at a place where successful people go to spend time. Business conferences. Real Estate meetings.

Trade shows. If you want to be surrounded by people who do amazing things, go to where amazing things are done. These groups frequently cost money to get in. Pay the price of admission. It is worth it.

The people you meet will be some of the kindest and best people in the world. Most people you see on stage are about the same person off-stage. They are all full of energy. Most of them are more focused on solving the world's problems than on making another dollar. If there was ever a guy that you would think would be loud or unapproachable it would be a Rock Star. I spent all day talking to a rock star at one of these meetings. I knew he was very successful if he sat at the table we were at. But I didn't know who he was. His name didn't ring a bell. Then I heard the name of his band and one of their hit songs. I couldn't believe that I had talked to him for hours and never knew that the #1 song that played on the radio at lunch was sung by the guy I was eating with.

Another Rock Star, in my opinion, the rock star of real estate, is Frank McKinney. I first saw him in person when he was on stage at the National Real Estate Summit (OREIA). I was working the back of the room and my kids were off doing whatever they do. Generally, that is sitting in the front row and asking very advanced questions. On breaks they are off networking. They always seem to be drawn to the most impressive and successful people in the crowd. The next thing I know, there is rock music blaring and this awesome intro playing. Everyone is getting in their seats except Deven. He is in the middle of the aisle recording with an iPhone. In runs Frank McKinney. I found out soon enough that they had met when Frank was walking in, and he asked Deven to record his entrance.

After this entrance you may think that Frank was unapproachable. Sure, he is surrounded by people, but when he is alone, he is completely focused on you. A few months later we were at his house. He was training for an ultra-marathon. He just had come back from his morning run, and we were saying goodbye. He spent the next hour or two talking to my kids. He had to make sure that they each got their own copy of one of his books. He gave us directions to the "Good Luck Circle." He told us how he walked his daughter to school every day. Her friends started joining them. I could see this huge group of 12-year old's listening to his stories on their way to school. They would have been as entranced as my 12-year-old was that morning. I imagined the lessons that he could have taught them in the fun stories he told.

I have always told stories to teach lessons. I find that people forget random facts, but they remember stories. If you mix emotions and experiences into your teaching, people get involved. It keeps the children's focus. And they retain a lot more of what we are teaching. This works on stage, and it works for a group of 12-year-old's. Since seeing how great Frank did this, I focused more on this type of teaching than writing outlines. I realized that I did do more story telling with my kids, and they were doing pretty well. I saw that Frank was a great storyteller, and he had achieved great results. Not just in business or writing, but with his daughter. If you do not know, she is incredibly successful in her own right.

I look at Mark Victor Hansen. When I first read *One Minute Millionaire*, many years ago, I just wanted to skip over the waitress's story. I thought "Just give me the facts." I want the outline to memorize so I know how to make a million dollars. By the time I was finishing the book I just wanted to know what happened to the kids. I should have learned back then that even an analytical mind like mine loves a good story. *(If you still just want the outline version, these lessons will be in an outline format in the end of each chapter of this book.)* After you read both versions, tell me what you remember more of. Now when I talk to Mark, he is always bringing up people. He is telling me how this person is working on world hunger. That one is going to get a million pints of blood to save lives. Frank talks about building entire hurricane resistant villages in Haiti.

All these incredibly successful people show you how they care more about people than anything else. They don't just say it, they do it. When you are with them you know that you are the most important person in the world to them at that moment. They are always gently pushing you to be bigger. To do more. To help others. They don't care how young or old you are. They definitely don't care about your gender or color. They just want to bring the world together. They want to make it better.

Every night I have told my kids to dream about making the world a better place. I believe if you think about something enough, if you dream about it, it will become a core drive of yours. It is the same reason we do affirmations. To teach ourselves that we are enough. That we can do difficult or even impossible things. All of us, including you, have the ability to change the world. So, make sure you change it for the better. Your kids are watching. They may not listen to you. They may not learn what you are attempting to teach. But they will always remember what they see you do. They will remember the stories you tell them. So, make sure they see you acting the way you want them to act. Make sure your stories are focused on the outcomes you want them to learn. Your actions and stories should be positive and inspire your children, staff, and friends to improve the world.

ERIC'S CHAPTER OUTLINE

- Be where you are. Focus on every single person you are spending time with.

- Why you want to do something is a much more powerful driver than just learning How to do it.

- Knowing Who can, and wants to, implement your ideas with you is the fastest driver of success. It is always about the people, never about the widget.

- If you go where successful people go, and have a positive high energy, you will draw the right type of people to you.

- Both children and adults learn and remember better if you teach them with stories. This activates their mental and emotional intelligences. The more of your intelligences you use at once (Mental, Emotional, Physical & Spiritual) the better you will remember and understand.

- When you focus on making everyone's life better, your life must get better so you can keep helping others.

- The most successful people in the world are constantly working on themselves and working to make the whole world better in some way. You can have anything you want if you help enough people.

LILA'S LESSONS

My family has been fortunate to have met and spent time with amazing and successful people. It all started before we had kids when Eric and I went to an event to hear Robert Kiyosaki and Donald Trump, two big names in real estate. At the end of that event, a guy got on the stage as the last speaker. Most of the huge audience had left, but there were still some of us remaining. The speaker's name was T. Harv Eker. We listened to him in awe. Those that left early missed out BIG time! We knew immediately that we needed to learn more from this man, so we signed up for his Millionaire Mind Intensive and, eventually, every other seminar that he had at the time.

Harv taught some of the events we went to, but he also had a few really good trainers, like Rob Riopel, David Wood, and Dennis Cummins, all of whom had a large impact in my life. Some events were multi-speaker events, so we got to hear from other great teachers, such as Blair Singer and Keith Cunningham. At the same time, we were going to other great seminars and events, including our local REIA events and the yearly OREIA Convention (now called the National Real Estate Summit), where we got to hear from other greats such as Jeffrey Taylor (Mr. Landlord), Marshall Silver, Pete Fortunato, and Vena Jones Cox.

Some of my friends at the time couldn't understand why we were spending so much money to go to all these different events. However, I knew I was getting so much more value out of those events than I ever got from school. Somehow, those same friends thought it was okay to spend tens of thousands of dollars going to college for a year, but the thought of spending a couple thousand dollars on a week-long seminar was bad. I tried to explain that what I was learning at those events was what allowed us to become financially free. Needless to say, I stopped hanging around those friends. They didn't understand me or support my choices, and I knew that they could only drag me down. I needed friends who would focus on what works and got me to my goals. I found those kinds of friends at these same events.

The biggest impact from all these seminars was a complete shift in how I thought about things. Many people read the book *Rich Dad Poor Dad* by Robert Kiyosaki and make comments about how it changed how they looked at money. These seminars changed not only my outlook on money but also investing, relationships, leadership, and success. I found that I could then look back and see how my thoughts and choices were creating my results. I realized how much I needed to adjust and think more positively.

For example, when Eric came home in 2003 and told me "Good news! I'm going to be a full-time real estate investor", I knew that he had lost another job. This made three in a row. I also knew that he didn't want to have a job again. At the time, I was irritated with how he told me and concerned with how we would make it all work. Now, I look back and realized that the way he approached it was exactly right, and it was the best thing that could have happened to us.

It's funny how life works out that way. If we expect something to be bad, it is. If we expect it to be good, it is.

Many people lose a job and think it is a terrible event. It becomes a time of struggle and frustration for them. Eric had decided that it would be a great thing for him...so, it was. It's like the quote from Henry Ford, which says "Whether you think you can or you think you can't, you're right."

The thoughts we allow in our mind create our reality. Our words become self-fulfilling prophesies. This means we must pay attention to what we think and what we say. We need to frame every circumstance in a way that benefits our mind. Harv would say that "Thoughts lead to feelings. Feelings lead to actions. Actions lead to results."

Gandhi said it slightly differently:
Your beliefs become your thoughts.
Your thoughts become your words.
Your words become your actions.
Your actions become your habits.
Your habits become your values.
Your values become your destiny.

Many great and successful people have made similar statements, including Margaret Thatcher, Denis Waitley, Hal Elrod, and Jack Canfield. This was a huge lesson for me, and I had to overcome a lot of negative programming in my own brain to understand how to start thinking positively. As I started to change the way I thought, I started realizing that my life was improving almost exponentially!

I started telling people, "I am naturally charmed."

Then, it seemed like everything started working out for me. From a logic perspective, I can look back on how thinking and saying that affected my beliefs and how I approached challenging situations. What was funny is that the people around me started to believe I actually was charmed... that somehow, some universal magic was at work! The only magic was in how I chose to think. You can use this same magic to improve your own life!

LILA'S CHAPTER OUTLINE

- Experience is the best teacher. Learn from people who have done what you want to do.

- If your friends do not support your growth and advancement, they are not your friends.

- If you know something bad will happen, it will. If you know something good will happen, it will.

- You have the ability to create everything in your life; in fact, you already have. If you want more, different or a better life, start by thinking differently.

- If you have trouble changing your thinking, just change what you say. If you tell yourself "I am naturally charmed" enough times, you will start to think it. You will start to believe it. And you will start to get the results of being naturally charmed.

CHAPTER 12

Trust & Let Go

ERIC'S EXPERIENCES

All of the Millionaire Mind Intensives I went to started with the same joke. The punchline was a guy hanging off of a cliff yelling for help, "Is there anyone up there?" God answered "Let go and trust." The guy yelled back, "Is there anyone else up there?"

It is amazing how many times you can ask for something, get it and then decide you don't want it exactly that way. I walked into one of my "Winner's Dinners," our Wednesday night meeting, and asked if anyone wanted to buy a house. The first question was obviously "How Much?" Then, just like almost every real estate class teaches, the investors at the table immediately responded with "Can I get owner financing?" I said yes.

They asked how much down. "One hundred dollars is fine." Someone wanted to know how many points on the loan. I said I would finance it with no points. But what is the interest rate they asked. I let them know that 10% was fine with me. They looked for another problem. Finally, someone asked how long until the balloon? I let them know that there was no balloon. I just wanted to make sure it was financed long enough that it cash flowed. If they made money, I was much more likely to get paid. They got all the answers that they wanted. Then, almost all these people who said they wanted to find a deal with owner financing went home and forgot about it or ignored it. Opportunity only knocks if you are listening.

Of the three people who did go to look at it, one said that it was too much work for them. I agreed that this was a decent rehab, and they may want to start with an easier one. Another said he already had one rehab going that he wanted to finish first. Also, a good idea. By then I wanted to see just how far I could go to make it an irresistible deal and still have people pass on it. So, I let him know that I would let him have it for a couple of months with no interest or payments. That way he could finish his other rehab and start on this right after that. He is a schoolteacher and didn't think he could get both done before summer break ended so he passed.

The final person looked at it and called me back. She asked every good question she could think of. I gave her the answers she wanted. She finally asked if she could use my contractors to do the work. I reminded her that the only reason I was selling was because I had bought a package of properties and my crews had way more work than they could keep up with. That was why I was selling a couple of the houses. She was meticulous in asking every question until she found the one answer that would allow her to say no to a deal. She is also the one who told me earlier today that she can never win. If you are wondering how can you find a meeting with deals like this, you may be asking the wrong question. The question is how many of these meetings have you already been to? Was there just one little thing off so you ignored a deal? Are you really looking for a way to grow your business or are you looking for a loophole so you can stay comfortable? I always look for a way to take something no one else wants and turn it into a deal. If it is perfect, it is probably already gone. But if you can find a way to make it perfect that no one else saw before, you can get anything you want in life.

At another dinner one guy asked me where I keep getting deals. Apparently, everyone believes that there are no deals in this market. He is right in some ways. I have not found any large apartment complexes at a good price listed by a realtor. If you work at it, you can find some deals. If you really work, you can find a way to make other deals good. And if you don't want to deal with the competition there are always other ways to get what you want. There are always smaller properties if you are willing to deal with the hassle of extra closings and having properties scattered all over the county. I told him about multiple landlords that I have bought out over the past couple years. I met some of them at the meetings I went to when I first started investing. Again, looking for any excuse to stay where he was comfortable, he decided he didn't want to wait for ten or twenty years for the people he was meeting tonight to retire.

If you want to see problems, you will. If you want to see solutions, you will. The property manager at the table, Lila, told him there are always disgruntled landlords at eviction court. Some of them would love to sell their properties that day. We discussed when and where court was held in each city in our county. All these new investors had to do was go there and talk to the owners after an eviction. It may be one of the best places to buy a group of properties all at the same time from the same seller. These landlords are also used to taking payments and frequently hate to pay capital gains taxes. That means that they are much more likely to finance the entire bunch for you.

For the parents wondering what this has to do with raising children, take them with you to court. There are so many lessons they can learn. Like pay your bills or you may lose your house. Or, said in a more positive way, make good decisions. Many parents tell their kids that bad things can happen if they do this or don't do that. We do not. We simply let them see the consequences of some decisions in real life. Another benefit is that you have your children with you. Some landlords that have done very few evictions will be very upset when they finish court. Kids change the dynamic of a negotiation. Your kids may even make them smile. Whether you buy a package or not, your family can learn things together and you may make the other land-lord's day better. It is also amazing how much these people are willing to teach the lessons it took them decades to learn to you and your child. If you meet someone who wants to talk, take them to lunch and enjoy the education.

One of my early mentors really seemed to have it all.

He had some land out in the country. He had 30-50 units and ran the real estate investment group for a while. He got to work with his wife and had some very intelligent and well adapted kids. We are still good friends today. His two sons grew up to be Marines, just like him. I still learn from him. And he still has the same life. Sure, it has improved in linear ways, but he still has to go to work every day if he wants anything to get done. That may be because he wants it to be that way. Some people are happy staying where they are. Others just make excuses and tell themselves that they want to be there. If you really want change in your life, you need to admit it to yourself and announce it to the world. You have to believe it with every one of your thoughts, feelings and actions. When you do, you will get the results you asked for.

I, like many of my mentors, can't imagine ever retiring to do nothing. I do not know if this mentor will ever really retire. Since he still has to, or more accurately, chooses to do manual labor, he may also choose to retire and relax for the rest of his life. The problem I see with this is most people who retire and do nothing, die within a few years. You have to keep your mind moving. You have to keep growing, even after retirement.

Most of my mentors have already "retired." Many of them multiple times. But they never quit learning and growing. We are just not that type of people. What is the use of being on earth if we can't keep learning, growing, and making the world a better place? I just choose to do it in more efficient ways. I do not want to keep working in the same ways I always have just so I could stay comfortable. I want to learn new ways, so my "Comfort Zone" constantly expands. While I want to keep working, I do not try to figure out how I can work harder or longer. I try to figure out how I can get more done efficiently. One way to do this is to hire more people.

When my previous mentor and I were talking, he brought up hiring contractors and employees. He told me that it is just him and his sons working in his business now. He just can't hire anyone that he can trust. I started thinking back fifteen years ago. He had to do all the work in the real estate group because no one else was there. He said no one else would volunteer. Multiple landlords that I buy out can't let go because "No one else will do it right" or "No one cares anymore." Thinking like this leads to burnout. That is why they sell all their properties, and their kids do not want to take them at any cost.

I look at the same job market in a different way. I have also found it harder to hire people than it was before. It takes longer. I set up interviews and they don't show up. I hire them, and they say they are so excited to start. Then the first day comes along and they are not there. You can't just give up on the world and accept that there is no hope when these things happen. You have to keep going until you find what or who you are looking for.

The number one thing I see holding people back in business, investing and raising kids is that they can't let go. You have helicopter moms that just hover over their children. You have self-employed people that quit or retire from a job just to buy themselves another job that they call a business. You have investors who find deals but don't buy them because they just don't have the time. All these things are done out of fear, doubt and worries about things that will probably never happen. If you want more out of life you have to trust more. You have to take chances. And you have to let go! If you already do not trust people to do it your way, you are destined to find employees that grow into that belief. If you don't trust your kids to order their own food because they won't do it right, you will get kids that never learn how to make decisions. Sure, they will order too much food. They will get food they don't like sometimes. But they also learn to try new things. They learn that they are in charge of their lives. They learn that the decisions they make have rewards when done correctly and punishments when they choose poorly. Wouldn't you rather your child order food you know they will not like when they are six than choose to buy toys rather than pay rent when they are twenty?

Once they learn to make these choices, they need to choose to take action. Deven always teaches to be Creative and Take Action. At dinner, I gave everyone there the creative idea of buying houses at eviction court. Lila told them when and where these hearings are held. Out of all the people there that night, no one said "I'll do that this week." If you really want to find a deal and someone gives you one, buy it! If you learn a new place to find deals, go there. If you want to stay in your comfort zone, then do that. Just don't expect to get any different results than you have been getting. I learned that you can lead a student to creativity but you can't make them take action.

When we focus on the How of a situation, we almost never get results. When you start by defining the Why, you will get a clear picture of where you want to go. Once you believe in your destination, you will find the how. The bigger the why you have, the bigger the how you will find.

Recently I realized that I was traveling a lot more than before, and while I kept growing the real estate business, I was not growing the construction business. In other words, I had bought more properties than my current staff could hope to fix up in any reasonable time frame. This started to create stress in my life that I did not want. I knew I needed to hire six more contractors to do all the work that was already lined up, and that was if I didn't buy any more rehabs until the current ones were finished and rented. I decided that rather than looking for six good maintenance and rehab people, I would just hire one more office person. Now she is my executive assistant, and she deals with hiring. I make it to the interview to approve them after the paperwork and background checks are complete. She has already designed a much better online application than the paper version I was using. The first person she hired may be the best person that has started in years. He resolved so many issues in the first day he had to call the office and ask for more work. I expect that we will have a long and prosperous relationship with each other.

Once you have good people working for your company, you need to keep them. One way I do that is to help them buy property. Some have never owned their own home. Others are ready to try owning their first, or next rental. Since I started investing, I have been asking everyone who works for me to come and learn what I do. I invite them to dinner every Wednesday. I offer to take them to lunch. I even have classes in the office sometimes. About half of them do end up buying a house for themselves. Some buy a few rentals. Last night I finally had one of my HVAC guys, Bill, show up to dinner. He has done work for us for about ten years. I am not sure why he decided to come last night for the first time, but I was happy to see him there. I don't care when you want to start. When you do, someone will be there to train you. He really reminded me how thankful I was for the great people we have been doing business with for years. I frequently use Bill as an example when I hire new people. Recently, when I was talking to the new guys about Bill, I realized how much our companies had grown with each other. These relationships are not only necessary for the growth of your business, but they also have a healthy and positive effect on your whole life and everyone involved.

****

BILL MELLOWS

Back in 2014 I was working a dead-end job at a sandpaper factory fresh out of school with an HVAC certification. A coworker just moved into a rental and asked if I could look at their furnace. I got the furnace going and when the maintenance guy called to come look at the furnace my coworker told him it was fixed by a friend. That maintenance guy asked for my name and number, and he hired me for maintenance and that's when I met Eric.

I worked for about a year with Clear Sky when Eric offered to sell and finance a house for me. It was the first house I ever owned. Eric has always tried to get me to come to his "Meetings" where he teaches about investing. I have been working for them for almost ten years now. My wife started working for their Real Estate Brokerage about seven months ago.

Eric and Lila started inviting her to go to the same meetings. It wasn't until then that we decided to go. I noticed a change in the way she acted. She had more confidence and felt better about life in general. After spending time with Lila and the other people in the office she was ready to try something new. We finally decided to start learning about investing. After a few months of going to their investor meetings we are now getting ready to start buying our own rentals. I finally understand how working towards financial freedom can change our lives. Not only do I have a "Secure job," I have started my own business. I've hired people to work for me. We are happier, healthier and starting our journey to financial freedom. All of this was made possible because we learned and took action on Eric and Lila's lessons.

— **Bill & Ginetta Mellows**

****

Always choose positive words and thoughts over negative. If you think that no one will care as much as you...you just haven't found the right people yet. If you think that no one can do a job as well as you, you will always be stuck doing that job. If you let go and trust people, you may get hurt. But you may also find new ways to do things that you never thought of. It is the Who, or the people, in this business that make it worth doing. You can see bad people. I just see people who made bad choices. And then I focus on the people who made good choices that have improved their lives and mine.

You can choose to do it all yourself. Or you can let go and trust someone else. They may prove to be better than you or they may not. Either way, you will be spending more time with your family and less time fixing toilets. If you choose to always do everything on your own, you will never be able to grow. Your children may learn that they always have to work long, hard hours just to make it. They may be the retiring landlords that are selling off their real estate to my children in another forty years. That is exactly what I wanted to prevent when I raised my kids. I decided to show them that this business can be fun. And it provides great benefits.

I choose to provide more jobs for the world. I choose to trust that there are good people who care as much as me. I know that there are many smarter people and more experienced people out there. I just need to find them and then provide a better life for them than their last job did. When searching for these people took up too much of my time, I just hired someone to do that for me. That way I get to spend time doing the things with my family that I want to do. At the same time my businesses are still grow-ing without me. What are the results of these choices on my business? I have more highly qualified contractors to fix my buildings. My new executive assistant is learning a lot and making my life much better. I have the resources to continue to buy more property faster. And on my family life? Deven just found out that another retiring landlord called me. He wanted to sell his last twenty-some proper-ties. Deven asked if he could buy four of this guy's prop-erties. The three of us are meeting tomorrow to discuss the terms of the sale.

While you may be the best you know, your business will never exponentially grow, until you let go.

ERIC'S CHAPTER OUTLINE

- We always get what we ask for. It frequently is not packaged exactly the way we think it should be.

- If you look for excuses to stay where you are, you will find them.

- If you don't trust yourself, you will never trust others.

- Great deals and great deeds are not handed to you. You must take an imperfect situation and find a way that no one else has to make it perfect for you.

- Children change the dynamic of a situation and a negotiation.

- Many retiring or burned-out landlords will sell all of their properties to you with owner financing. This is one of the best ways to buy more faster.

- Living things are either growing or dying. There is no standing still.

- To grow out of your current "Comfort Zone" you have to let go and trust.

- You can lead a student to creativity, but you can't make them take action.

- Align yourself, your family and your business with others who want to grow, and you will all grow faster together.

- Hire people for anything you do not want to, or do not like to, do. There are people who will like every part of the business that you do not like.

- If you are the best you know, you will never exponentially grow, until you let go.

LILA'S LESSONS

Getting your first real estate deal under contract is both an exciting and nervous moment. Eric and I had evaluated and purchased the first few deals together. Then, to get more done, we started to divide the tasks. I focused on doing the painting, cleaning, minor plumbing, and management of our current properties. Eric did the purchasing, financing, and all the other rehab work. We took every opportunity to implement as many lessons as we could from the meetings and seminars we attended and the books and courses we listened to.

One of these lessons was to have a team working for you. It was difficult to let go and trust someone else. We weren't sure if they would do a good job. For some tasks, we didn't even really know how we wanted them done, so how could we explain it to someone else? We knew that we needed help, so, we started hiring out some of the easier tasks that we didn't want to spend time doing, like mowing and cleaning. While it was uncomfortable at first, we realized that this was making our life much easier and better.

As we started hiring more, this lightened my workload, and, in order to continue to provide value to our partnership, I returned to the task of looking for deals, even though for more than a year I had relied on Eric to do all of the purchasing. I started some short sales and practiced working with banks, just like I was learning from a course we purchased. In 2005, I got my first short sale approval from a bank. My nerves kicked in, as I felt out-of-practice purchasing properties. Another investor approached me and really wanted to purchase that property. They said they were happy to pay me a wholesale fee for it. This was a relief for me, because I was nervous about closing on a property, on my own, without Eric helping me. I happily assigned that contract to the other investor. That made us a few thousand dollars, but I knew that we really needed to be adding to our own portfolio. Then I found a motivated seller in another city. This would become my first deal purchased and held that Eric would not see until after it closed.

This first deal on my own might as well have been my first deal ever. It was just as exciting (and nerve-racking) to be doing all the same steps with no one there to help. I found a little 2-bedroom home that was a forty-minute drive from where we lived and got it under contract. This was going to be our farthest property, but, while not as convenient to get to, it had a good location. I found my own financing from a hard money lender at our REIA. I negotiated him down a percent in interest as well as getting him to waive the points. My goal was to buy the home, fix it up, and refinance it, so I only needed the financing for a few months. I thought I was doing well figuring out things on my own.

Then, after it closed, Eric walked through it. He explained that because you had to walk through one bedroom to get to another, it was really only a 1-bedroom home. He told me the stairs, which had a part where a tall person would have to duck going up them, would probably detract a lot of tenants. He told me that I was going to waste a lot of time driving to a property that far away. He also told me that I should have figured in the cost to replace all the carpet because, while it was in great shape, it was an ugly olive-green color. Changing the carpet would blow my entire budget out of the water. Suddenly, I wondered if I had made a terrible mistake in buying this home.

However, I wasn't giving up. I completed the renovation, including having a new roof put on. I used some dye to change the carpet color (which I later found out would only make it through one tenant but did make it look better). I completed the refinance and got it rented. Over the years, this home has broken every expectation. It seems to attract good tenants who stay for a while. It doesn't sit vacant for long when they do move. The city it is located in has turned out to be great to work with. Since then, we've bought a lot more properties in that area. This potentially "bad" deal has turned out okay. Talking to other experienced investors, I learned the decisions you make with a property make a big difference. You can turn a good deal bad, and you can make an OK deal good. I learned a lot from this deal, including some things to watch for in buying future deals. The most important thing this property did was to teach me that I can buy properties on my own and figure out how to make them work. It gave me the confidence to go do more. I was glad that Eric trusted me to do all of this without his input. It built my confidence, and now we both make sure we do the same for our children.

Now, I watch other people getting started investing, and I feel their discomfort. I can remember being there. Many new investors seem to avoid taking action because the deal is never perfect enough. Most people don't understand that the first deal will always be their worst deal and their best deal. It is the worst because they don't have enough experience... yet. New investors are bound to make a few mistakes... just like I did. Even if you do make mistakes, you have plenty of opportunities to improve the deal if you catch the mistake quickly enough. The first deal is also their best deal, because it gets them started and gives them the confidence to do more. It takes courage to get through the first deal. One way to make the first deal easier is to find a mentor. Then you can use their experience. Trusting in them and yourself, is one of the most important things you need to get started.

In order to handle fear, first you must recognize its existence. Those getting started investing always seem to blame something else – a deal not being good enough, the market not being strong enough, or some other external factor that is just not "perfect" right now. At the same time that they find excuses to keep them from having to take action, even though they see other investors are buying and enjoying the benefits of their actions. There is never truly a perfect time or a perfect deal. Sometimes circumstances can make things easier, but in the long run, it is better to be moving forward all the time, even if circumstances are not "perfect". In order to do that, we need to acknowledge our fear and then determine how to lower the number of mistakes and risk. Again, asking a mentor for help is a great way to do this.

Finding a mentor means having to ask for help. Some people have a difficult time doing this, including Ethan. He is a very strong-willed person who believes that he can achieve anything. While this can be great for powering through a challenging time, it can make it difficult for him to admit when he needs help and to ask for it. On one level, he understands that there are times that he needs help. However, he gets involved in brute forcing through a problem and doesn't stop to think about how he can make it easier or more efficient. Asking for help does not make you weak. It makes you smart. No one succeeds spectacularly on their own. The most successful people always have a team of people that help them on a daily basis. They understand that this help is crucial to success. This is why many people will quote that TEAM means "Together Everyone Achieves More." Children are already learning this when they are in sports, dance, theater or other group events.

Robert and Kim Kiyosaki say that, when it comes to investing, the first thing you should do is get some education. The problem is, once you have been taught something, you will not automatically understand what they taught until you take action and practice the lessons. The goal is not to spend thirty years "educating" yourself without taking any action on what you've learned. It is not to know everything before you start your business. It is to learn something, and then practice it. Then, learn something else and practice that.

Eric and I knew after spending so much money on education, we had to make it count. While we were going through the Peak Potentials seminars, we completed a class at least every month. Every time we came home to work, we immediately implemented at least one of the lessons we had learned the week before. At times, we were in a class every other week. No matter how short the time was between classes, we always implemented at least one thing we learned before we went to the next course. It was hard… and worth it.

Educating yourself is important. It is important to choose what you want to invest in, and then spend time learning about that type of investment. You need to trust yourself to take action and move forward by practicing the lessons. When you need it, ask for help. As you grow, build your team. Then trust them to help you succeed. It all starts with that first deal…while you are developing the ability to trust and let go.

As a parent, learning to trust our children and let them do things on their own is very important. At conferences, Deven and Ethan frequently want to watch different speakers than I do, so they go off on their own in a large crowd of people. I do not walk with them but trust that they will find their way to the right room or ask someone for help. It is difficult for a parent to let go and let their children do things on their own. We want to protect them. Some parents try so hard to keep their kids from having any bad experiences that they go overboard in that protection. Their kids either expect everything will get done for them or they rebel just so they feel like they have some control. It is better to give them the opportunities to practice being responsible for themselves, so that as they grow up, they will be ready to handle themselves and be on their own. As parents, we need to trust and let them go.

Another important time to let go and trust is when you are forming a team. Of course, you need a system and guidelines...but you can't control everything. You need to tell them where to go and then trust them to find the way there. You have to trust in yourself that you hired the right people, and you have to trust in them to get the job done. Then, verify their actions and results regularly. Too many people are afraid to hire people because they don't want to let go and trust. However, they usually don't want to be the only one doing every task either. These are the people that usually get burned out in business or real estate. To succeed, we need to be able to let go of our fears, trust in ourselves and our team, and then watch carefully to make adjustments and corrections when needed.

You need the courage to act. You need to implement what you are learning as you learn it. Then, trust yourself and your team to make that deal the best it can be. These steps are not comfortable in the beginning, but the more you do these things, the easier they get. Then, you will see others getting started and feeling their own discomfort, and perhaps you will be able to help them learn these lessons.

Life is about more than book knowledge. It is about facing our challenges and fears with courage. In the end, it is the actions we take that determine our future.

LILA'S CHAPTER OUTLINE

- To grow, we divided and conquered our workload.

- The more we hired others, the more we could grow.

- When you trust yourself or anyone else to do something, new mistakes will be made. Just identify and overcome them. That is when you grow.

- No property purchase is a good deal or a bad deal. Your decisions make every deal good or bad.

- Every deal you learn from is a good deal.

- Getting a mentor is a great way to shorten the learning process.

- Building a team is crucial to the success of your business and your family.

- Don't get stuck with "Analysis Paralysis." Learn something; then practice it. Repeat...

- If you do not trust your kids or staff, they will either never learn responsibility or they will rebel.

- Give them the goal and let them choose the path.

CHAPTER 13

Words Have Power: My Word Is Law!

ERIC'S EXPERIENCES

My Word is Law! Nothing is more important to me than my word. I have built a business based solely on my word. Every promissory note I have ever signed was my word and my bond. I did not hope to pay my lenders. I promised to pay them. My purchase agreements were not a way to tie up a seller's property for as long as I could, with as little as I could for earnest money, just so I could find a reason to back out after wasting their time. They were agreements to purchase. When I say I will be there at 10:00am I will be there. When I sign a purchase agreement, I will close. When I sign a promissory note, I will pay. My earnest money says that I am earnest. And when my kids ask me to play with them, I play. I do not go through the motions while I am thinking about work. I am very careful with the words I choose.

A few years after I started investing, I bought my first mobile home park from a couple of very experienced investors. It was also my first property over fifty units. One of the investors, Joe, threatened to walk out at a couple of times in the negotiations. I saw that Ray was playing the "Good Cop" and Joe was put into the positions of "Bad Cop." I think he was supposed to be getting me to cave in some way, but I really just saw my dad or another drill sergeant. I knew that I had trained hard so my life would be easier. I also knew that both of them had way more experience and knowledge than me, so I listened and learned. A couple years later I helped my bookkeeper buy another mobile home park from them. Then I bought that park from her and took over payments to them when she realized that owning something like that was not for her.

Each time I got to work with Joe again. He was always the tougher one, but he was always fair and knowledgeable. Many years later I paid off both of these parks at the same time. They still held the financing. Joe called me and told me that he didn't always agree with me but there was one thing he respected. I always did "Exactly what I said" whether he liked it or not. He then told me that if I ever found a deal that was too big for me to handle on my own to call him. He would be happy to be my partner. That meant the world to me. I have had many great and successful people tell me that they would be happy to partner with me. Every time I hear this I am honored. I know exactly what that means. I know how much I have to trust and respect someone before I would be willing to partner with them. To hear this from someone who was always on the other side of the negotiating table as I meant even more. It meant that no matter what our disagreements were and no matter how much we wanted to get more out of the other party, we both always acted with respect. This is just one of the benefits of being true to your word.

Words have power. Harv says "Thoughts lead to Feelings, lead to Actions lead to Results."

The bible says, "And the word became flesh and dwelt among us." I can tell you that there is no better way to activate the law of attraction than to call out what you want over and over. Repeating the same affirmations everyday will give you what you ask for. If you say "I can't win" … You won't. If you say, "Why does this always happen to me?" It will keep happening. If you say I have plenty of time to do everything I want, You will.

You can read all kinds of books that tell you that positive affirmations work. Once you see that is true, you will also see that negative affirmations work as well. Be careful what you think. Focus on exactly what you say. You will have bad thoughts. You will be negative. That is not the problem. It is not even how many times you think negatively. What matters is how quickly you can reframe those thoughts as positive. If you really want to accomplish more in life. If you want to raise better, healthier, wealthier children, you just need to train yourself to quickly remove the bad/negative/scarce thoughts and replace them with good/positive/abundant thoughts, words and actions.

I still do not understand why people promise to be somewhere at a certain time and then show up late. I know there is traffic sometimes. Pretty much every day during rush hour. Every possible contingency can be planned for and mitigated. The worst excuse I ever get is something like "Oh, it's OK. She is always late." Or "That's just who

I am." If that is just what you do, it tells me everything I need to know about you. I know that how you do anything is how you do everything. I will never lend money to a person who is a minute late to a meeting with me. If you don't respect my time, you don't respect me or my money. If you are late to a meeting, you will be late on your payments.

I was contemplating buying an apartment complex with a new partner. I had decided that the complex was a good deal and would cashflow after we repositioned it. When he thought I was evaluating the complex, I was really evaluating him. After seeing the choices he made all day I invited him to my home. I wanted to verify what I had seen all day in a more controlled environment.

I told him Friday was game night and asked if he wanted to play Cashflow 202 (from the Rich Dad company) with my family. As I watched him play I noticed multiple things. First he threw his money in a pile. He never knew what he had there. He didn't respect his money. That is one of the reasons he needed me to bring in all the money to the apartment deal in real life. He kept saying that he wanted passive income but would only take capital gains deals. Just like real life. He had been a Realtor for years, even before I started investing, and now, decades later he thought he was ready to buy an investment property for himself. After seeing how incongruent his choices in the game were, I chose not to partner with him on this or any other deal. I wished him luck finding financing for the deal and told him that I would help him with contractors and contracts when he needed them. He ended up never buying it.

Some people show up to meetings and say, "if you're not 5 minutes early, you are late". That does not mean that I will immediately do business with them. But it is a great start. It shows me they respect my time. Even more than that, it shows they respect their own time. I do not want to be in business with someone who constantly wastes time.

I had a partner who told me over and over that his time did not matter. He thought it was a good thing that he would give freely to our company. I knew that eventually he would resent that he was working for free and I was not. This could have become a serious issue so I wrote into our initial agreement that any work either of us did would be paid for. He is a great person. He is helpful. He has time that he gives freely because he is retired. He has accomplished many great things. He is still a good friend, but we are not partners anymore. We want different things in life. When I wanted to grow and learn, he was not ready yet. Now I am moving far too fast to slow down, and he is finally ready to get started. I want more long term growth. He wants more quick results.

Sometimes you can find good people who could be good partners but you are just in different stages of life. That is what happened with him. He wanted the same things as me but at different times. So, I introduced him to another one of my friends, and they bought a small apartment building together. I hope that partnership grows way bigger than ours ever did. I hope they both get exactly the type of rewards that they want. They both deserve it. I would be involved with either of them if our goals aligned at the same time.

The way I see it, is that you can have a good deal. You can bring in partners or team members that have all of the traits and qualities you are missing. You can have clear communication and use the exact words at the exact time to convey the meaning you want. And sometimes things still do not work out.

Imagine how hard it would be for a child to understand all of this when you are intentionally misleading them. "If you don't look both ways you will get hit by a truck." What if they run across the street and don't get hit? Did they just learn that you intentionally lie to them? Did they learn that mom and dad are wrong? What if you try to cover it up and say it was just a little lie? It was for your own good.

It is either all true or it is not. If you justify that you are just doing it for their good, you are still lying. If my wife asks if she looks good in an outfit, I tell her the whole truth. If you have to lie to keep your marriage, you should look at what else you have to tell yourself that may not be completely true.

Do not yell at your kid that he is a bad boy. He may grow up to be one. When he does something wrong tell him he made a bad decision. Tell him he did a bad thing. Mistakes do not make us bad people. No matter what the school system says. They just help us learn to do things in a different and possibly better way. When your son, daughter, or staff makes a poor choice, tell them. When they get poor results, talk about it. Do not hide your head in the sand like an ostrich and hope everything fixes itself. It almost never does. When you and your partner's goals change, identify and fix it before it grows into a real partnership-ending problem. If your children are integrated into your business, they will see this and learn how to handle changing times and changing people for the rest of their lives. Even if they are not, they will see how you and your spouse learn and grow together or how you grow apart. Don't just tell them, show them how to be the great leaders, teachers and people that you want them to grow up to be.

My parents got a divorce when I was a teenager. When my mom bought a new house I immediately stepped up and mowed the yard. I fixed everything that broke around the house. I hung all of her many pictures and cabinets in this new house. I even grilled out when mom wanted food on the grill. I keep saying that "I" did this. But "I" would never have known how to do any of this unless I had watched and learned how to do it before that time. Now I watch my wife come home from the office and ask why her team can't seem to get a certain task right. She eventually figures out that she also has trouble with that same task. They are watching her and learning from her actions, just like I did. Just like our kids are doing. I watch Deven make the same mistakes as his mother. Then I look at Ethan. My strong, and stubborn younger son. I watch him refuse to ask questions. He has to use brute force to prove he can do anything his older brother or dad can do. Then I realize exactly where he got that from. He is just like me at that age, and like I still am now. It is so easy to see what everyone else is doing that holds them back. It is so hard to see it in yourself!

Some people go to church or pray for understanding. Others spend 40 years meditating in a cave. I focus on the words that people...especially me, use. While it may be hard to see what you are doing wrong at the time, it is amazing how easy it is to record a conversation you had and then see exactly where you went wrong. You can sit down and write or type how you want a negotiation or even a vacation to go. Doing this slows your mind down enough to see your inconsistencies and where you are not congruent. It is even better if you have people around you that will always tell you the whole truth. If your family and friends think, Like Col. Jessup said, "You can't handle the truth," perhaps you should question why they are hesitant to tell you the whole truth. And when you do find someone who will always give you the whole truth, especially when it is not flattering, keep them around forever.

Do not pick a partner, spouse or mentor just because they make you feel good all the time. Pick one who makes you want to be good all the time. One who always wants to help you improve yourself, your team, your family and your life. A mentor should always build you up, not tear you down. And sometimes, they need to tell you where you are messing up so you can fix it and do better. When you become that better person that you want to be, you will do better things that you want to do. It is not the success in life that make us great. It is the challenges in life that give us the strength and power to become successful. Your partners, mentors, friends and family should be there to drive you when you are moving forward and to help you up when you fall. When you surround yourself with people like that, you will have the better life and family you want to have. Your kids and staff will watch this and some of them will also want to be, have and do better. Help them. Teach them. Mentor them and show them. Lead by example. Then, start working on yourself again so you can be, do, and have what is waiting for you on the next step of your life.

ERIC'S CHAPTER OUTLINE

- Perception is reality. Your reputation is who you are.

- Even if you are not exact with the words you use to ask for what you want, the universe is exact with giving you what you asked for. Choose your words carefully.

- Look them in the eye and tell them exactly what you mean. They may not like the information, but they will respect your honesty.

- Your words will turn into real things. The more you say something, good or bad, the more it manifests in your life.

- You need to train yourself to quickly remove your bad/negative/scarce thoughts and replace them with good/positive/abundant thoughts, words and actions.

- If you are late, it is not just a couple of minutes. It shows a lack of respect for your counterparty and their time. Why would anyone want to work with someone who did not respect them?

- If your actions do not match your words, no one will believe you.

- Even great people may not be great partners for you if their goals are not the same as yours.

- If you justify a "Little Lie" with a good reason, it is still a lie.

- If you have to hide part of the truth from your partners, it will go wrong.

- There is a big difference between being a bad person and accidentally doing a bad thing. When someone on your team or in your family messes up, be clear in the way you address the problem. If they respect you, they will grow into your estimation of them.

- It is much easier to see other people's issues than it is to admit what your issues are to yourself. Let others help you with this.

- Business and relationship partners are not there to always make you Feel good. If you choose the right one, they will always make you, and help you, Be good.

LILA'S LESSONS:

If the people that know you were to describe you, would they say that you are dependable and trustworthy? Or would they say that you are always late and frequently make excuses? When you make a promise to someone, do you make sure that you fulfill it, even at great personal sacrifice, or do you make excuses so you can back out if it gets too hard?

How well you hold to your word determines your reputation. If you want to build your credibility, you need to make sure your actions reflect the characteristics that give you a good reputation. You must make good decisions, and if you make a promise, you need to fulfill it. If you schedule an appointment, you need to be on time. If someone is depending on you to accomplish something and any unexpected problems occur, you should communicate these immediately, so both sides are aware of what is going on and can agree on a solution.

Deven learned at an early age how important his reputation was. He knew he had to build his own credibility over the years. He learned that his words and actions not only created his results, they would build or tear down his reputation. Mom and Dad's reputation opened the door, but the moment he walked through, he was on his own.

He started working on his reputation when he was young and going to investment meetings. Many people were not sure what to think seeing a young kid at these meetings. However, they also saw him paying attention, taking notes, and asking intelligent questions. Some people would talk to him and be surprised at how much he knew. Some of these investors ended up working with him by selling him a property or even financing his deals. They were impressed with his knowledge, dedication, and communication. He got financing for his first deal based on the deal itself. The small hedge fund looked at the amount of equity in the deal and agreed to loan the money. Deven made sure that every monthly payment was made early so that he could build a good reputation with that lender. Then, he knew for his second deal, he would have at least one reference to use that would say how perfectly he paid. After his second private lender, he had another reference. He built his reputation for following his agreements and having a perfect payment history.

Ethan had a similar experience. He followed agreements and had a perfect payment history. He also developed a reputation for being a good negotiator. I remember walking into the room while he was talking to a seller, and all I heard was him saying, "Well, putting the new windows into that home is going to cost $2000, so would you like to put in the windows before we close or would you prefer to just discount the purchase price by $2000?" This was a valid question. The seller had his own maintenance crew, and Ethan needed to know what the seller wanted from the deal. The next day the guy that was selling the property came into my real estate office to tell me about the negotiation and how impressed he was with Ethan. He couldn't believe that a 9-year-old was negotiating with him like any adult would. In the end, they had come up with an agreement that worked for both of them, and this investor enjoys telling the story about his negotiation with Ethan.

Following through on your word is not only important in business, but it is essential as a parent. If you tell your child that you will be at their baseball game to watch them play, you need to be there! If you aren't, not only will they be disappointed, they may learn lessons you don't want them to learn. They may think that whatever you were doing was more important to you than they are. If you tell your child that if they don't clean up their room you are going to take away their video game system, do that. If you don't take it away, you have now taught your child that you do not follow through on your word. The next time you tell them something, they may take it as an idle threat rather than a promise. What is worse, if they see that you frequently do not follow through, they will not respect you. You need to be clear when communicating with your children and follow through on any promises.

When Deven and Ethan were little, my mom would come in the spring to visit us at our house every year. Then, close to fall, we would take her on a trip to somewhere fun with us. Since she lives many states away, this allowed my kids to visit with her twice a year. In 2014, there were problems that led to many flights getting cancelled from her local airport. She called us to say that she wouldn't be coming as planned. This did not go over well with the kids, who wanted to see Grandma. In order to keep our promise to our kids that they would get to visit with Grandma, we all loaded in our Cessna 182 and flew to visit her, which was a long flight in that airplane. She got to show the kids where she lived and what the local museum was like. We all had a great time, and, most importantly, the promise of getting to see Grandma was fulfilled. If there are circumstances, or other people that cause you to break a promise, find a way to change the circumstances. Then, you can keep your word, even if it is in a different way than you originally planned.

Any team who chooses to work with you will learn these same lessons by watching your actions. They will learn if they can count on you or not. If I promised a reward when my team met a goal and then I didn't fulfill that reward when they met it, they would quickly lose respect for me and would be much less likely to put forth much effort toward the next goal. However, if they know that whatever reward is offered will always be given, they will work harder to achieve the goal and win the prize. Over the years, I have offered rewards, contests, and special events when goals are met. It has made some difficult times a lot more fun. I always record these on our whiteboard, so that everyone has the reminder of the bonus and can monitor their progress to achieving it. My team knows any reward on that board will always be given if they meet the goal. Giving the reward when they don't meet the goal, even if they are "Really Close" also ruins your credibility. Your family and your team need to have exact and measurable goals. They need to know that there are rewards for meeting them and punishments, or at least a lack of rewards, for missing them. Being dishonest to make someone feel better never makes you, or them, a better person.

When my real estate company needs maintenance done, we always hire outside contractors to get the work accomplished. Some contractors have told us that they will not work for a management company because they had a bad experience with other companies that did not pay them. I have also called a new roofer, who the minute heard our company name, knew that we always paid in full weekly. We had asked him how much he needed down for materials to get started on a particular job, but he said "You're Clear Sky. I've heard how you pay. You don't need anything down. I'll have this roof done by Friday and I'll come in the next week to pick up a check for the whole job." We ended up working with that roofer for many years. It was our good reputation of always paying in full, every week, for any completed job that helped start that great relationship. It was his word and always meeting deadlines that kept it going.

Your word needs to mean something. People need to be able to rely on what you tell them. So be true to your word. Build a good reputation. That reputation will help you go farther faster. If you have problems keeping your commitments, today is the day to change that. Make the decision right now who you want to be and what kind of reputation you want to have. If you want to have the reputation that you always do what you say and are great to work with, then make every action reflect those characteristics. Be the one who is on time, on task, reliable, respectful, cooperative, provides value, and communicates effectively. Who you choose to be will affect who wants to work with you. If you want to work with amazing and successful people, you need to be the type of person that they choose to work with.

You choose who you are. Your decisions and actions define you. Make decisions and take actions like the person you want to grow into: the one who achieves what you want to achieve. Then, you must commit to being that person all day, every day, in every thought, feeling and action that you take. Your words and actions must be congruent. Every thought, word and action must get you closer to being that perfect image of who you want to be every day. Once you have that clear image in your mind and your actions reflect it, you will find that your results will begin to improve and bring you closer to your goals. You will find the people that you want to work with will be drawn to you, and you will see new opportunities available to you. So, the question is: Who do you want to be?

LILA'S CHAPTER OUTLINE

- You are either the person that does what they say at any cost, or you are the person who has an excuse for everything. No one can be both.

- When you do break any promise, take responsibility immediately.

- When your words match your actions, the sum of these parts become your reputation.

- No one gets by on anyone else's reputation for long. Start building your own right now.

- Using logic and respect, a 9 year old can effectively negotiate with an experienced investor.

- Follow through on all of your promises or people will not respect you.

- There is always a way to keep your word. It may not be the way you originally planned, but there is a way.

- Being dishonest to make someone feel better never makes you, or them, a better person.

- Your word always means something. Make sure it means what you want it to.

- Choose every thought, word and action carefully. Make sure each one gets you closer to goals you want to achieve.

CHAPTER 14

··

Think Big & Take Action

LILA'S LESSONS

What do you want out of your life? What do you want for your business or for your kids? Many people do not get what they want because they do not have clarity on What they want. They will say generic things like "I want to be happy," but happiness is an emotion that a person chooses – not a destination or goal. Goals have specific, measurable descriptions with time frames. It should be easy to see if you are on track, and easy to know when you have achieved your goal. Once people do define a goal, most only ask How they can accomplish what they want. In order to achieve your goals, you need to know Why you want it. What will drive you to reaching your goal? The stronger or more important this "Why" or driving factor is, the more likely that you will succeed in achieving the goal. What you also need to ask is Who can help you to achieve the goals? No one succeeds spectacularly on their own. Everyone needs the talents and knowledge of others to get there. Build a team and maintain good relationships with people. Have the courage to ask for help when you need it. If you do not ask the question, you can never get a "yes." While not every question may get you that answer, it is not possible without asking.

Most people want the freedom to live their life how they choose. Homeschooling gives parents the freedom to teach their children the lessons that they believe are important for their kids to learn, in the manner they want those lessons taught, in any location they choose to teach them. Business and investments give people the financial freedom to go where they want, when they want, with whomever they want to spend time with. Many people want this freedom but get stuck on believing that they need safety and security. These things are not freedom. You need to believe in your own ability to assess risk and make your own decisions. Then you will not need anyone to provide you with safety or security. Then you will be truly free.

Help others to improve their lives by making better decisions and accomplishing their own freedom. Whether it's your children or the people working for you, they need to practice evaluating and making good decisions. Responsibility can only be learned if you have freedom of choice. Anything else just fosters dependency, and the goal of both a parent and a business owner is to have your kids or staff learn to work independently. Both sides need to be able to see the Big Picture and how they fit into it. You must trust your kids or your team and empower them to do things for themselves. Otherwise, you are the bottleneck in the process that is preventing success. Trust, let go, and then verify their results to make sure that they are on track.

Success does not happen overnight. As Ray Kroc said,

"I was an overnight success all right, but thirty years is a long, long night."

Even Steve Jobs said, "Overnight success stories take a long time." Do not get discouraged if your success is not as fast as you were hoping. Know that every lesson and every step to success is just part of your journey. These are the moments that you will tell stories about later. The most difficult times that you overcome are the ones that will allow you to help someone else overcome similar challenges later. The more difficult the journey, the more rewarding the completion.

We need to acknowledge how much power our thought processes have in creating our results. We need to be very selective with the words we use both in our communication to others as well as our own thoughts. Every word our mind takes in, turns into something real and physical. If we focus on and talk only of the bad situations in life, we will find ourselves in more bad situations. We need to focus on the positive thoughts that lead us to a better life. How we think, speak, and act will create our results. If we don't like our results, we need to reevaluate our current beliefs. We can only achieve what we set out to do when our thoughts and actions are in line, or congruent, with our goals.

To become successful, people need to grow themselves to be bigger than any problem that they may face. It takes courage and strength to grow. Too many people settle into their own mediocrity and say that they are "comfortable." This only holds them back from achieving greatness. We all have a talent or skill to offer to the world. If we hide in our own comfort, the greatness within us remains trapped.

Matthew 5:14-16 of the Bible reads "You are the light of the world. A city set on a hill cannot be hidden. Nor do people light a lamp and put it under a basket, but on a stand, and it gives light to all in the house. In the same way, let your light shine before others, so that they may see your good works..."

Marianne Williamson said that "Our deepest fear is not that we are inadequate. Our deepest fear is that we are powerful beyond measure."

I believe that many people feel overwhelmed by the thought of doing something new, even if it allows them to share the best parts of themselves with the world. They hide under their own blanket of comfort, and that greatness within them is lost to the world.

We need to accept that somewhere within us is something so valuable that not only do we have the ability to give it to the world, we have the duty to do so. It will not be comfortable. It may be terrifying, exciting, and, at times, frustrating when the journey to deliver your value to the world isn't as smooth or easy as you'd like. It will challenge you, exasperate you, and motivate you. To bring this value to the world, you will have to grow yourself beyond where you are now and perhaps even beyond anything you can image in this moment. There will be moments when you jump to the next level and can run full force toward success, and there will be others in which you will face a mountainous obstacle that you need to overcome. It will be your perseverance, positivity, and team that will move that mountain out of your way, so that you can jump up and start running again. You need to believe in yourself to achieve anything. You must accept that the value you have to offer the world is so important that you must make the journey.

As Dr. Seuss says in *Oh the Places You'll Go* (*with a minor change as I used to read to my kids):

> *And will you succeed?*
> *Yes! You will indeed!*
> *(98 & ¾ percent guaranteed.)*
> *Kid, you'll move mountains!*
> *So...*
> *be your name [Deven or Ethan*] or Bray*
> *or Mordecai Ali Van Allen O'Shea,*
> *you're off to Great Places!*
> *Today is your day!*
> *Your mountain is waiting.*
> *So...get on your way!*

When Eric and I had children, we wanted to teach them the lessons that would allow them to grow, be self-sufficient, and to discover and deliver their value to the world. They have accomplished these things earlier than anyone expected. I believe it is because we taught them to be limitless – to be free of any self-imposed limitations. Eric and

I had to overcome many self-limiting beliefs before we could succeed. Deven and Ethan started without these. Homeschooling is what gave us the ability to achieve this with our children. Our results are what are driving us to share this with the world, so other kids can learn what they aren't getting from traditional school and reach their own early success. The traditional school system is focused on standardized tests rather than knowledge that will help the students for the rest of their lives. This is like a business that is focused on short term cashflow and not long-term growth. I want today's kids to be prepared to achieve success throughout the rest of their lives. Traditional school teaches kids as if they are all the same. They are not. They learn differently and they think differently. This is a great thing. As parents and leaders, we need to encourage these differences. We do not need to standardize our children.

I believe our differences are what allows us to achieve such amazing results. Different ways of approaching a problem are how we develop new solutions. This means we need a team that is comprised of people with different perspectives. We need people that think and do things differently; people who have the creativity to do something new. We need to work with these different types of people so we can all achieve great results.

We aren't all the same, so our learning can't always be exactly the same. The learning methods should be tailored to address the different needs of students. This can be achieved in one room. T. Harv Eker was great at using music and spoken words for the auditory learners; demonstrations, colorful drawings, and written lessons for the visual learners; and experiential practice for the kinesthetic (or action) learners. We incorporated different methods like this to give our kids what they needed while they were learning. We created a system for teaching our kids that produced great results. If our system can help other families achieve great results, then we want to share it with the world.

We believe that everyone should be a student and a teacher. We should learn from our own experiences and the people who have done what we want to do. Then, we should take what we've learned and teach it to others. We taught our kids the lessons that have brought them success. Now, they share these lessons with other people.

Integrating our business and investing with our family life was the best choice we could have made. It has made life exciting and rewarding and has given us many stories to use to teach others. If your family wants to learn these same lessons, we can help. We look forward to hearing your success stories as you make your journey!

LILA'S CHAPTER OUTLINE

- If you are not clear on what you want, you will not get what you want.
- Have a specific, measurable, goal with a timeframe for every aspect of your life.

- Having your own business, investments, and home-schooling your children gives you freedom. Having a job and sending your kids to school gives you the illusion of safety and security at the expense of freedom.

- Responsibility can only be learned if you have freedom of choice.

- We can only achieve our goals when our thoughts and actions are congruent with our goals.

- You are enough, open yourself up to the world so it can benefit from your genius.

- Success is like a staircase. Sometimes it is like running across a flat meadow. Then you hit a mountain. It takes perseverance, education, and a team to get you over the mountain to the next step so you can run again.

- The only limitations in the world are the limits you place on yourself.

- The strongest groups and teams are always comprised of different types of people with different ideas working together for the same goal.

- All lessons in school, business and life should have auditory, visual and kinesthetic parts.

ERIC'S EXPERIENCES

I never had a problem taking action. I hated waiting. People will tell you the most miserable I have ever been was when I was bored. I also wanted more out of life than many of my friends. The people I worked with would tell me things like "Slow down, you're making us look bad."

"Why do you want to be rich? I just want to be comfortable."

I always tried to think at the level above where I was. I dressed for the job I wanted, not the job I had. In the Army I trained to replace my supervisor and was ready at any time to do just that. When we first started our business, I told everyone that I was already a millionaire, the world just had not seen fit to give the money to me yet. I acted as-if I already had it. I attempted to make decisions like I would when I became successful. I also imagined what a perfect father would do and then attempted to make the decisions that would allow me to grow into that role. For a while I thought I was doing pretty good. Then, thinking I was a big fish, I left my little mud puddle and went to a bigger pond. After almost getting eaten, I found the big fish in that pond. They became my mentors. I realized how my "Big thoughts" from before were really the things that were holding me back.

Then I recognized my core beliefs, the ones I thought made me so successful, like always taking responsibility, were also the things that held me back. Of course, I took responsibility, I would not trust anyone else to do part of my business. It is the duality of our beliefs that both get us ahead in life and hold us back. I worked very hard to separate the positive part of taking responsibility from the negative part, not letting go. You should never blindly trust anyone. You need to look at the data in every situation at every time and make your own informed decision. Ronald Regan said "Trust but verify." Times change. Situations are a little different. And when we open our eyes and really want to see the big picture it is always right there. I just had an uncle tell me "Who knows what the truth is. It is so hard to tell who to believe." I find it very easy to know who to believe. I believe in me. I believe in facts. When people's actions are congruent with their words, I am more likely to believe in them. If someone says one thing and does another, they are not trustworthy. Only you can decide when to let go and trust. Just because someone is called an expert does not make them right. Even if they are correct in some circumstances, it does not mean that their advice is the best advice for you right now. You have to step-up and make the decision that is best for you right now. You have to take responsibility for the outcome of your decisions. And you need to teach your children and your staff that it is okay to do those same things.

Never be afraid to change your mind. If there is new evidence that makes your old opinion invalid, you must come up with a new hypothesis. And if people constantly flip-flop or change back and forth without any evidence, they are not trustworthy. The problem today is not finding enough evidence to support a theory. You can "Prove" anything you want if you cherry-pick the facts that support your beliefs. This can make you happy and keep you comfortable. When you want to grow you have to start looking at more facts. Before you can think bigger you have to accept that the facts you know for sure are exactly the facts that are keeping you stuck right where you are. Part of these "facts" may support your growth while the other side of the same "Facts" may be your biggest obstacle. If you want to grow, you have to let go. If you want your kids to do better than you did on this planet, if you want them to have a better life, be more successful and to raise a happy, healthy family of their own, you have to stop teaching them your self-limiting beliefs. None of us can do this until we stop telling everyone how to get to their goal. We need to learn to help them define their goal. We may even help them get the vehicle they need to get to their goal. Then we have to let them choose their own path to get there.

When I teach my children something, I don't tell them exactly how to do it. I tell them what needs done. If they are totally lost, I tell them where to start. Once they have the beginning and the end of a task defined, they can decide what path to take to get there. If you are always there to tell your kids what to eat, what time to go to bed and exactly how to mow the yard, you are taking away their freedom. What is worse is you are depriving them of the practice that they will need to make good decisions when you are not there to help. Every time you tell your staff to do it the right way or punish them for trying something new you are destroying their creativity. As long as your goals are measurable and have a time frame you will be able to see if your way, the old way, is better or if they just found a new better way to accomplish a task. Once you have respect for and have built the trust with your family and your colleagues, it is time to see what they can do without you. Every tall building is built on a solid foundation. First build that foundation with your team and then see how high your team can go.

When you raise your children to be responsible and show respect to others you can trust them to make the best decisions at the time. Of course, they will mess up. Of course, they will do things differently than you would have in some situations. These choices are what build our character. Later in life they will have to be part of a team other than your family. These other teams will be evaluating them to see if they have different skills and traits that can benefit the new team. Some of them will be the leaders who put the teams together. They will be the ones who choose what different strengths are needed to succeed. There will be plenty of highly educated and specialized people to choose from. And there will be very few that can step back and see the big picture. The leaders will always be thinking bigger. They will constantly take on bigger tasks and want to create more. They will not let fear prevent them from taking action. And their actions will match their thoughts and words. Train your kids to be these leaders. Empower your staff to grow your business. Once you have a group of people who want the same goal as you, give them the freedom to achieve that goal.

When Lila and I started this journey, we started building

a business. We used that to start investing. Our investments grew our business. Then we had children. We decided to teach them about business and investing. We saw that the traditional school system not only did not have financial education, it actively worked to destroy the traits you need to be successful in business and investing. We refused to teach our kids about freedom and responsibility and then send them to a place that made them memorize the one right answer. Seeing this contradiction allowed us to see the contradictions in our own business. This helped us to become more congruent. The more we taught them, the more we learned ourselves. The more we grew, the more mentors we found. These great people never taught me how to do anything. They taught me to see why something needed done. When I grew enough to move to an even bigger pond, the mentors showed me who was doing what I wanted to do.

When I was a kid, just like Ethan, I was very proud that I could do these things on my own. I never need anyone's help. I went so far down that path that I actually became an instructor for survival in the Army. Now I realize that self-reliance is the positive side of that coin. Not being able to trust the people who can help you grow is the other side of that same coin. It is hard to differentiate the parts of the lessons we have learned. It is not always clear what part of the lesson allowed us to succeed and what part held us back. Open you mind. Think bigger. Be creative and keep taking action. These are the only ways you will grow into a bigger, better person. These are the things that will allow us all to make the world a better place.

Respect the people around you. You will not always agree with anyone. When you respect the people you disagree with the most, you grow more respect for yourself. This will allow you to forge stronger relationships with your family, your friends and many people you have not even met yet.

I remember sitting in some random hotel talking to Stewart Welch when he told me to "Think Bigger." I remember reading Frank McKinney's book Make it Big. Now I am working with Mark Victor Hansen who is Relentless. Every one of them has told me in different ways to think bigger and help more people. They have also put me in touch with the people in this world who can help me achieve my goals. It is not the How; It is the Who. Successful people don't act the way they do because they are successful and can afford to be. They are successful because of their thoughts and their actions. They are great givers. They really do care about you and all of humanity. It is wanting to make the world better that helped them become successful.

The synergy of my family gives me the strength to accomplish the things that I do in business. These accomplishments allow my family to spend more quality time together so we can create more synergy. Once you see that your life is stuck in a positive feed-back cycle, I hope you will make the decisions that allow that cycle to drive you forward rather than hold you back. When you do, you, your family and colleagues will have such an advantage over everyone trying to do it on their own that you will never want to go back to the "Old way." Use this momentum to build a great team with different strengths. Create a system that makes your business, your customers lives and the world better. This team is the leverage you need to grow exponentially bigger and better. Don't ever let fear or any other negative emotion hold you back.

Don't ignore an opportunity because it does not look the way you want it to. People say that history may not repeat, but it rhymes. You may not see an opportunity because you think you know what it should look like. Open your mind. Take in the whole picture. Be open to any opportunity, no matter what form it takes. Grow physically, mentally, emotionally, and spiritually until you are big enough to recognize these opportunities. No living thing can stay the same. We are always growing, or we are dying. You are always becoming more of something. So, make the choice to be something good. A positive force in the universe. Be grateful for all that you have earned and are given. Then take that and turn it into more so you can have a better family life. Create the environment that allows your kids to grow up stronger in every way. Take that environment to work with you so everyone there chooses to grow with you. When your friends question why you want to grow and change, question if they really want what is best for you or if they are just trying to keep you safe. Take advice from those who have already done what you want to do.

Not from your friends who are living the same lives that you want to grow out of.

Only you can change your life. Only you can choose both, business and family, success and happiness, generosity, love, and money in every situation in your life. You will never earn enough money to be happy. But you can choose to be happy today. Trust me, it is much easier to create wealth when you are happy. Do not confuse the cause with the effect. Just because things are correlated, or happen together frequently, does not mean that one causes the other. Look for the facts. Make your own decisions. People can show you creativity, but they can never make you take action. Remember that you will always get what you ask for in life. Why not ask for more? You are exactly the person that your decisions from the past few years have created. You are a mixture of the people you have chosen to spend time with. And five years from now you will become the person that your thoughts, feelings, and actions create. You are either the person that does what they say at any cost, or you are the person who has an excuse for everything. No one can be both. A reputation is a fragile thing. No one gets by on anyone's reputation for long... even their own. Whoever you are today, wherever you are today, you can change and grow into whoever you want to be. Start building your bigger and better life right now. Choose every thought, word, and action carefully. Make sure each one gets you closer to goals you want to achieve. Choose your team and the people you spend time with carefully. You will become more like them, and they will become more like you. Give your family the gift of freedom. Let them choose. Let them make mistakes so they can grow. Learning always happens. Make sure they are learning the lessons that will support them and help them to grow.

The world is changing faster than ever. We have more information in our hand every time we pick up a phone than most people could ever have imagined just 50 years ago. We have the internet, spreadsheets, and social media. These things are making the world smaller. They are also making our worlds much bigger. We can hire a Virtual Assistant from another continent. We can be a VA for someone in another country. There have never been more opportunities to make your life better for so many people on earth. People are thinking so big and moving so fast that 50 years from now I may write about the opportunities in the solar system or even in the universe rather than just on this little planet. All of these things can be used for good or bad. You can generate enough electricity to power a city and make a million lives better with a nuclear reactor. You can also take a million lives away with a nuclear bomb. Lila's company uses an internet-based software that allows her office staff to know exactly when a maintenance issue is completed, who did the work and what was done. Another version of this software allows millions of hours to be wasted spreading negative ideas on social media. The worldwide integration that should be drawing us together is being used to push us apart. The tools are not good or bad. It is how we use them that creates good or bad results. We, as human beings that all share the same Pale Blue Dot in space, need to focus on integrating the positive and abundance into our lives. Only then can we share it with others. The more we learn to work together, the more abundance we will create on this planet and the next. There has never been a time in history that we have had more of EVERYTHING than we have now. It is time that we took these great resources and used them to build a bigger, better future. It is time to quit hiding from change and growth just so we can stay safe and secure...or even comfortable. It is time we questioned our self-limiting beliefs and stopped passing them on to the next generation. Today is the day we all need to take action to make this world a better place!

ERIC'S CHAPTER OUTLINE

- Take action now. The bigger the action, the bigger the results.

- Act, dress and talk as if you are already at the next level, and you will be soon enough.

- Always be thankful for what you have in life, and then go strive for more.

- Core beliefs are like coins. One side gets you ahead, and the other keeps you where you are. You have to see both sides so you can learn to separate these positive and negative parts.

- Whether you take responsibility for your decisions

or not, you will live with the outcomes of those decisions.

- If new evidence makes your opinion invalid, you must come up with a new conclusion

- Most of our self-limiting beliefs were taught to us by the people who love us the most.

- The more you grow, the less you will focus on How something gets done. You will see Why it needs done, and then you will see Who can help you do it.

- Opportunities rarely look the way we think they will.

- All living creatures are either growing or dying. Make sure you are constantly growing mentally, emotionally, physically, and spiritually.

- You have created the life you have today. Accept that all of the bad and all of the good is your creation. Then go create more of what you want and what is good for the world.

- No matter who you are or where you are today, you can change. Make sure your thoughts and actions get you to where you want to be in a few years.

- The more we learn to work together, the more abundance we will create on this planet and the next.

- It has never been easier to grow. Now is the time. So, Think Big and Take Action!

Epilogue

I wanted to make sure that my sons did not end up being like the Ericksons in the *One Minute Millionaire*. Now I know with all this great support around them they never will.

I wanted to grow a business and not miss any time with my family. Not only have we made games out of business tasks, we created a whole new business that allows us to travel together and grow together.

I wanted to make sure not only could my children run a business, if they ever lost everything, they could rebuild it. And most of all I wanted to make sure they remembered to have fun every day of their life. I knew they could learn and do all of this at the same time they were making the world a better place. They have proved me right. Now you just need to believe if we can do it so can you!

We did not believe that the traditional school system would help our kids grow into the adults that they could be. Since we started homeschooling it has become much more popular. We created our courses to teach them what we thought they would need in life. We never tell them to sit down and be quiet. We teach them that they can get much farther if they work as a team. We teach the fundamentals of starting and growing businesses, not how to climb the corporate ladder.

As we became more successful, others saw that success and asked how we did it. This book is not just the How. It is the Why we did it. It is our experiences, including Who helped us along the way.

Many people want to change the school system. Others like it how it is. The more a system divides and holds back its students, the more new systems will emerge. As more people choose alternative ways to learn, more systems will be created. We are teaching one of these new systems. When one, or many of these new systems working together, proves to be far superior to the traditional system there will be change.

In Robert Kiyosaki's newest book, *Capitalist Manifesto*, he talks about the traditional school system teaching communism. He says that we need to teach capitalism at home. This is what we did for our children when we saw the problems with the traditional school system. This is our system for teaching capitalism at home.

Our goal was just to give our kids the best chance at a good life as we could. What emerged was a very different way of teaching from the traditional schools. When I saw how many other people were embracing new ways of learning I knew that the world was ready for a change.

It is our hope that the lessons in this book will add to the new system. A system based on abundance and teamwork rather than scarcity and division. We, as parents and business owners, do not need to fight the old system. We simply need to build a new system that is so much better than the old one, that the traditional system becomes obsolete.

— Eric M. & Lila J. Wohlwend, 2022

"Never doubt that a small group of thoughtful,
committed citizens can change the world.
Indeed, it is the only thing that ever has."

—Margaret Mead

OTHER BOOKS FROM OUR FAMILY:

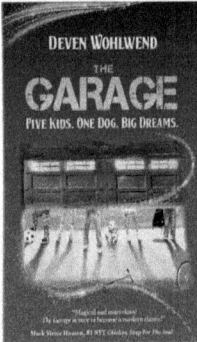

Look for other books from our family that use fictional characters to teach the same lessons from a kid's point of view. In *The Garage* series Atlas Gold invents new ways of solving problems… Despite meddling by the mayor, who wants things to stay as they are.
By Deven Wohlwend

Available on Amazon - https://rotf.lol/garage

In *The Treehouse* series Darius Knight and his friends build a treehouse to play in. When they use their new skills to help a couple people around town, they end up with a new handy-man business.
By Ethan Wohlwend
Available on Amazon.

About the Wohlwends

Ethan A. Wohlwend, Eric M. Wohlwend, Lila J. Wohlwend, and Deven J. Wohlwend

Eric and Lila have been a full-time Real Estate Investors since 2003. They received both the Ohio and the National Professional Housing Provider certification in 2006. They specialize in being creative to make deals in any type of market. They have repositioned more than a thousand units. They still control hundreds of single & multi-family residential properties as well as many types of commercial property. They have spoken in five countries, on three continents and in countless states. They have written multiple articles in various Real Estate Investment newsletters and published a bestselling book on leadership.

The Wohlwend's have used millions of dollars of private money from more than 100 private lenders to finance their real estate deals. Eric finds creative approaches to make good deals great and Lila manages the properties to make them even better. They use systems for management and operations to maximize value.

Their kids, Deven, now fifteen and Ethan, who is currently twelve years old, both bought their first piece of real estate when they were seven years old. Neither used any money or credit from their parents. Deven published his first book when he was eleven. He has been interviewed on many podcasts listened to in more than 190 countries and has spoken to live audiences in more than half a dozen states. Deven's companies currently own over forty-five units. Deven is a #1 Best-Selling Author of *The Garage* and *If I Can Do It So Can You-How I Started Buying Real Estate at Age 7*. The second book in his Garage series *The Fall & Rise of Atlas* will be available this winter.

Ethan's company owns over thirty-five units and he recently started speaking. He has also been on multiple podcasts including Rich-Dad Latino and The Real Estate Guys. Ethan's first book *The Treehouse* will be published in 2022. Each of these books teach the lessons about business and investing that made the family so successful.

The family has recently fought overreaching governments from the city to the federal level. In 2020, when the CDC declared that landlords could not evict, they took on the CDC. This family, and some fantastic lawyers, beat the CDC in the Cleveland federal court. This helped to restore the rights of all property owners in the US.

When they are not buying more real estate, the family

travels the US, Canada and Mexico in one of their private planes training other investors to do what they are doing. They speak on Creativity, Action, Management, Arbitrage, Systems, Private Lending, Homeschooling, How to Take on the Government, and many other topics. In their free time, Eric and Lila continue to homeschool their two children. The whole family travels everywhere they can to learn, teach and spend time with other like-minded individuals, like you.

If you would like more information about the Wohlwend family, their free newsletter or their companies' services you can visit www.ClearSkyTrainer.com.
On social media they can be found @RealPowerFamily.

Eric M. Wohlwend
Lila J. Wohlwend
Deven J. Wohlwend
Ethan A. Wohlwend

CPSIA information can be obtained
at www.ICGtesting.com
Printed in the USA
JSHW011157190223
37772JS00003B/166

9 798885 810746